Luciano Bellosi

GIOTTO

SCALA

CONTENTS

The illustrations in this volume have been supplied by
the SCALA PICTURE LIBRARY,
the largest source of color transparencies and digital images of
the visual arts in the world.

The over 60,000 subjects visible at the site
www.scalarchives.it
can be accessed through computerized procedures that permit
easy and rapid picture searches of any complexity.

e-mail: archivio@scalagroup.com

The images from the SCALA Picture Library reproducing cultural
assets that belong to the Italian State are published with the
permission of the Ministry for Cultural Heritage and Activities

© Copyright 2003 SCALA Group S.p.A.
Antella, Florence

Photographs: SCALA Picture Library
except no. 101 (Gemäldegalerie, Berlin), no. 120 (National Gallery,
London)

Printed in Italy by: Amilcare Pizzi S.p.A.-arti grafiche
Cinisello Balsamo (Milan), 2004

Early Works

For most people Giotto is the first name in European painting since antiquity. That he had breathed fresh life into painting was recognized by his contemporaries, and later by Ghiberti and Vasari. He had "that art which had been buried for centuries by the errors of some who painted more to please the eyes of the ignorant than the intellect of the wise," wrote Boccaccio (some ten years after the artist's death) in a tale of the *Decameron*, in which he stressed both the physical ugliness and lively wit of "the best painter in the world."

Before Giotto, painting was still considered a craft, a "mechanical" art. Giotto came to occupy a position of great respect in Florence, a city that was one of the most important centers of trade and commerce in Europe. He was representative of that spirit of rationality and efficiency typical of the Florentine mercantile class of the time. Though he was employed by the Bardi and Peruzzi families, owners of the most important European banking houses of the day, he never limited his activity to Florence, and prestigious commissions in other parts of Italy kept him constantly on the move. He worked at the basilica of San Francesco at Assisi, then one of the most prominent churches in Christendom; for the pope; for Enrico Scrovegni, the richest and most influential citizen of Padua; for the king of Naples; and for Azzone Visconti, the *signore* of Milan. He also provided the high altarpiece for St. Peter's in Rome. At a time when Italy's flourishing economy made every Italian city an independent cultural and artistic center, Giotto transcended regional barriers and the impact of his art was felt throughout the peninsula.

He was born in about 1265, and must have been active before the last decade of the thirteenth century. The first clear signs of the nature of his artistic revolution are to be found in fresco decorations in the Upper Church at Assisi: the Old Testament scenes starting with *Isaac Blessing Jacob*, the vault decorated with the *Doctors of the Church*, the New Testament scenes including *Christ Among the Doctors* and the *Lamentation*, and the St. Francis cycle. Despite the lack of knowledge surrounding Giotto's formative years, these frescoes can be considered the turning point of his early career.

Not everyone agrees that they were conceived and executed by the artist who later painted the frescoes in the Arena Chapel in Padua. Indeed, some feel that the Assisi frescoes were merely influenced by Giotto's art, that they were painted after the Paduan frescoes, or that they are a product of the Roman school. These views were first advanced by art historians of undoubted competence and are still held by many.

It is unlikely that the Assisi frescoes were painted after those at Padua. Space does not permit me to go into detail, but I shall give one example. If we consider the small angels (or would it be better to call them angelic spirits?) that appear in scenes such as the *Lamentation* and the *Confession of the Woman from Benevento* in the St. Francis cycle, we notice that they are cut off at the waist and terminate in drapery. This is in complete accordance with thirteenth-century iconography, and can also be seen in paintings by Cimabue. This detail, then, would appear to date the Assisi frescoes to a pre-Paduan period, and other details link them more specifically to the style of Cimabue.

There is a tendency to overlook the link between Giotto and his great Florentine predecessor, Cimabue. If we compare the Paduan and Assisi frescoes, we notice the difference between the softness and fluidity of the former and the sharp incisiveness of the latter, which gives the drapery an almost metallic appearance while the colors seem almost transparent.

Cimabue, from the destroyed *Crucifix* in Santa Croce to the *Evangelists* in the vault of the crossing of the Upper Church at Assisi, had employed similar "transparent" color. In this respect his *Madonna and Child* in the collegiate church of Castel Fiorentino is particularly close to Giotto's frescoes in the Upper Church. Duccio, whose style was, in part, derived from the work of Cimabue, had borrowed the splendid chromatic subtleties of his *Rucellai Madonna*, now in the Uffizi, from the Florentine master. This use of color in Giotto's Assisi frescoes separates them in time from the Paduan ones. It also suggests a parallel between Giotto's early activity and Duccio's development, from the transparency of color in early works like the *Rucellai Madonna* of 1285 to the chromatic density of his *Maestà* in Siena, painted between 1308 and 1311.

Giotto was probably working in Assisi by about 1290, more than a decade before he started on the Arena Chapel. The St. Francis cycle was probably painted at about this time, though it is usually dated after 1296 (Vasari records that the cycle was commissioned by Giovanni da Murro, who only became general of the Franciscans in 1296). This is not the place to examine the reason for this dating. Suffice it to say that Cimabue's influence, mentioned above, plus the suggested parallel with Duccio's painting, and the irreconcilable stylistic differences between the Assisi and Paduan frescoes can be only explained by the existence of a long interval between the execution of the two cycles. The difference between the St. Francis and Paduan cycles is much greater than that between the St. Francis cycle and Giotto's other fres-

1. View of the nave of the Upper Church at Assisi with the Legend of St. Francis

2. The north transept of the Upper Church at Assisi with Cimabue's frescoes

3. Detail of Giotto's decoration of the Upper Church at Assisi

coes in the Upper Church. This indicates that the interval between the St. Francis and Paduan cycles must have been much longer than that between the St. Francis cycle and the other Assisi frescoes.

In spite of the impression of unity created by the Upper Church frescoes, those by Giotto are easily distinguished, not only for their style, but also because they display a completely new concept. That fresco technique had changed radically by the time Giotto began work on his frescoes is evident from their state of preservation. The disastrous condition of Cimabue's frescoes (already noted by Vasari) is due to his faulty use of pigments and to the old practice of plastering as large an area as the scaffolding would permit. Giotto painted on several relatively small patches of plaster, as large as could be comfortably painted in a day. As the plaster was always wet, the pigment penetrated deeply and uniformly, ensuring the preservation of the colors. In this way only the final touches had to be painted on dry plaster, whereas the method used by Cimabue required large areas to be painted *a secco*, (i.e. when the plaster was dry).

However, the technique was not the only novelty, since the very conception of the fresco had changed drastically. Cimabue and his contemporaries had regarded the wall as a surface to be covered with two-dimensional representations. The decorations around the margins of the pictures were conceived as flat ornamentation, similar to that of a tapestry or miniature, and included large plant motifs, ribbons and other ornamental elements painted in flat, bright colors. But Giotto's frescoes create the impression of being framed by the very architecture of the church, and the scenes are represented three-dimensionally, as they would appear in the real world.

The walls on which the scenes of the life of St. Francis appear, which project out slightly beyond the upper part of the wall, have been decorated with painted mock architectural elements. These begin with the painted curtain running beneath the scenes of St. Francis and culminate in the simulated architectural framing of the scenes. Each bay of the nave is divided into three sections (four in the case of the wider bay nearest the entrance) by twisted columns rising from the base, painted so that they appear to project above the architrave.

So resolute was Giotto's desire to impose this system of architectural illusionism that when the mock framings meet the projection of a real rib descending from the vault they are seen to slant downwards when viewed from the side. The fact that the same framing appears to be perfectly horizontal when viewed from the center provides a valuable indication of what the artist considered to be the ideal position for looking at the frescoes.

The scenes of the life of St. Francis appear to be set in space behind the mock architectural framework, which has been painted to look like part of the walls of the church. This gives the effect of peering into a series of small rooms, and calls to mind Leon Battista Alberti's concept (when discussing painting in the fifteenth century) of the surface of a painting as an open window through which we imagine we are seeing what is represented.

The scenes are planned according to principles of perspective that were first formulated in the two scenes from the life of Isaac on the upper walls. In these frescoes the delicate yet rationally articulated architectural setting creates a space that is clearly defined: the pale ocher sheet, whose edges are clearly detached from the bed underneath it; the partly drawn curtain and the horizontal rods that support it, one in the foreground, the other in the background; the foreshortened side wall with its oblique opening; the light-colored columns in the foreground; the small windows in the dark wall at the back; Isaac's halo, which blocks out part of the head of the servant who

supports him from behind. The space thus created is very shallow, but it is just this constriction that makes it seem perfectly measurable. The effect of coherence is heightened by the disposition and treatment of the figures, whose solidity is established by the gravity of their attitude, the depth of the folds in the clothing, the strong modeling and the single light source.

There can be no doubt that such a coherent conception of space was regarded as an innovation, and that it was a discovery of immeasurable value to the future of Western painting. It was just this methodically constructed space of the Assisi frescoes that met with immediate and widespread acclaim, first in Italy and then abroad, especially from the second half of the fourteenth century.

Giotto was prepared to eliminate unnecessary complexity for the sake of putting his new ideas into effect with maximum clarity and consistency. His painting is much less ornate than that which preceded it, especially when compared with the intricate, teeming compositions of Cimabue and the young Duccio, who with their cold, transparent colors sometimes achieved extraordinarily soft and ethereal effects. By contrast, Giotto's painting is much simpler and more succinct, despite the many sculptural folds that characterize the drapery in his early frescoes, a legacy from the classical-style drapery of thirteenth-century painting.

The concept of space evident at Assisi had been known to the ancient world, and lost in the Dark Ages. But it was not merely a question of a new way of painting. The idea of reconstructing three-dimensional space illusionistically on a two-dimensional surface restored importance to that reality perceived by the senses which had been lost in the intervening

4, 5. *Isaac Blessing Jacob and detail of the scene
depicting Isaac Rejecting Esau
Upper Church, Assisi*

years, when the only true reality was considered to be
that of the spiritual world. Giotto's reversal of this
concept paralleled certain trends of thought, especially prominent among Franciscan intellectuals, that
were to culminate in the Nominalist philosophy of
Giotto's English contemporary, William of Ockham.

Giotto's architectural settings are not merely a
means of creating pictorial depth, but also a reflection
of contemporary Italian architecture. At times they are
reproductions of real buildings like the Palazzo Pubblico
and the Temple of Minerva in the Piazza del Comune at
Assisi, both of which appear in the *Homage of a Simple Man*. The mosaic inlays which decorate the architectural structures in his Assisi frescoes, and which sub-
sequently became commonplace in fourteenth-century
frescoes, are nothing more than reproductions of the
Cosmati work made by Roman marble workers
throughout many parts of central and southern Italy.

Giotto's capacity for renewing the art of painting
by observing reality through his own eyes becomes
even more impressive if we consider the number of
Byzantine conventions which were then firmly rooted
in Italian painting. As prescribed by the Orthodox
Church, Byzantine painting was based on the repetition
of preexistent models and on faithfulness to established
formulas. For the architectural setting of a "sacred story," Italian Byzantine painters resorted to stereotyped
structures like the dome-shaped baldachin, evidently
of Eastern origin. Even in representations of the *Leg-*

6. *Mosaic with Angel*
San Pietro Ispano, Boville Ernica (Frosinone)

end of St. Francis, which was more or less contemporary, and certainly not Oriental, the Berlinghieri family of painters and other thirteenth-century Tuscan masters had frequently used such pictorial clichés.

With Giotto's frescoes at Assisi, this tradition was discarded, together with pictorial formulas of an abstract significance, intended as reminders of a reality different from that of this world. Still present in the art of Cimabue and the young Duccio, these were banished by Giotto, and the painting of human beings regained a more normal, earthly appearance and a naturalness whose only immediate precedent can be found in French cathedral sculpture.

Christ's heavy body in the Santa Maria Novella *Crucifix*, which was soon to become a basic prototype (in 1301 Deodato Orlandi was already copying it in his *Crucifix* in San Miniato al Tedesco), is of such earthliness that some have considered it unworthy of being attributed to the sublime artist of the Arena Chapel frescoes. Yet the work is so much in keeping with the ideas Giotto was developing at that time in his Assisi frescoes that the figures of the mourning Virgin and St. John in the side panels are almost interchangeable with those of Esau and Jacob in the scenes of the *Story of Isaac*. The two groups of figures have enough features in common for us to be certain that they were conceived by the same artist: the wide, square shoulders; the intense gaze (sorrowful, as befits the occasion, in the two Florentine figures; slightly clouded by a melancholy reminiscent of Cimabue in the Assisi figures); the solemnity and stiffness of attitude; the many fine folds in the classical clothing; the ears shaped to

resemble the handles of an amphora; and, in the figures of the Virgin and Jacob, the nose flattened to form a sharp angle, the cheek defined by the shallow cavity that begins at the nostrils and the high cheekbones. Ghiberti cites the *Crucifix* in Santa Maria Novella as a work of Giotto's and a document of 1312 records a crucifix by Giotto in the same church.

These figures also bear a striking resemblance to the two half-length figures of angels, one at Boville Ernica and the other in the Vatican Grottoes, which are the only remains of Giotto's most famous work: the mosaic of the *Navicella* (*Christ Walking on the Water*), designed for the facade of St. Peter's in Rome and almost completely remade during the seventeenth century, following the reconstruction of the basilica, begun by Julius II in the sixteenth. The similarity is apparent in the old-fashioned way of draping the cloak over one shoulder.

After the two scenes of the *Story of Isaac*, the frescoes in the Upper Church at Assisi continue in the bay nearest the entrance. The work began, as was the custom, in the vault, where the four *Doctors of the Church* are depicted, and probably proceeded along the upper walls in the large lunettes flanking the windows where scenes from the Old and New Testament are arranged on two levels. Of the Old Testament scenes, the two of Joseph (*Joseph Cast into the Pit by His Brothers* and *Joseph and His Brethren*) in the lower tier are still partially legible, while there remains only a fragment of the scene above, the *Death of Abel*. The fragmentary New Testament scenes include *Christ among the Doctors*, the *Baptism of Christ*, the *Lamentation* and the *Resurrection*. This series is concluded on the entrance wall with the large scenes of the *Ascension* and the *Pentecost*, which are surmounted by tondi with busts of *St. Peter* and *St. Paul* and surrounded by a series of full-length figures of *Saints* arranged in pairs on the soffit of the entrance arch. The saints stand within lovely mullioned shrines painted illusionistically using the same technique that was to be applied to the framings of the *Legend of St. Francis*.

Since the frescoes in this series are not up to the standard of the two Isaac scenes, they are probably the work of the artists who later assisted Giotto in painting the *Legend of St. Francis*. The difference is especially evident in the scenes of *Joseph and His Brethren* and the *Pentecost*, the fresco of *St. Ambrose* on the vault, the bust of *St. Paul*, many of the figures of saints and the small busts of saints on the soffits of the two arches linking the vault to the side walls. But here, too, the treatment is faithful to the new vision that first appears in the *Story of Isaac*. Looking at these frescoes, one gets the impression that Giotto's ideas have been interpreted in a somewhat archaic manner, (especially in the fresco of *St. Ambrose*), and in the apparent reluctance on the part

7. Crucifix
578x406 cm
Santa Maria Novella,
Florence

8. The inside of the façade of the Upper Church at Assisi

of the painters to abandon abstract pictorial formulas of Byzantine origin (see the small busts of saints), a less convincing solidity of figure (see *Joseph and His Brethren*), and an excessive attention to detail in certain parts (see the figures in the *Pentecost*).

Yet most of the frescoes maintain a dramatic tension and pictorial incisiveness that places them on a level with the scenes from the story of Isaac and the *Crucifix* in Santa Maria Novella. Certain aspects of these works are of a very high quality indeed: the intensity of expression of the young Christ among the doctors; the solemn expression of grief in the *Lamentation*; the profound, concentrated gaze of St. Peter in the tondo; the remarkable foreshortening of the sleeping soldier in the *Resurrection* (strongly reminiscent of the foreshortening used in the figure of the

9-11. Joseph Cast into the Pit by His Brothers;
The Cup Found in Benjamin's Sack; Lamentation over
Christ's Body
Upper Church, Assisi

friar kissing the saint's hands in the *Death of St. Francis* in the Bardi Chapel of Santa Croce); the acolyte who writes at the saint's dictation in the fresco of *St. Gregory*, (the same face, the same air of melancholy as in the figure of Jacob); the imposing composition of the *Ascension*, where Christ, who has Isaac's slender, tapering fingers, is borne aloft on a cloud which is both soft and yet strangely rock-like.

The frescoes of the entrance bay are so fragmentary that it is difficult to evaluate the innovations in composition and spatial experiments first seen in the *Story of Isaac*.

Nevertheless, a few words should be devoted to the *Doctors of the Church*, which are in a good state of preservation. Each of the four learned men is accompanied by his acolyte, and above each pair is a bust of Christ, framed in a cloud. Following the model of Cimabue's four *Evangelists* in the vault above the altar, the various objects represented in each fresco are made to converge towards the vertex of the triangular field. It is almost as if the artist had attempted a kind of view from below upwards, and therefore incorporated the convergence towards the vertex into the foreshortening.

The chief interest of these frescoes lies in the fact that for the first time in the history of painting they represent the polychrome effects of bright marble, inlaid with mosaic decorations and embellished with colored molding, which had been used on the facades of the most important churches in Central and Southern Italy, and in their furnishing – ambones, episcopal thrones, altars and tabernacles.

So great were Giotto's interest in physical reality and his capacity for expressing it in painting that even his wooden furniture assumes an amazing, almost *trompe-l'œil* tangibility. Some of the objects are depicted down to the last detail, as can be seen in the writing desk of St. Gre-

gory's acolyte, and in the scroll on which he writes, where even the two eyelets in the paper are shown.

One is reminded of the panel painting, clearly the same *Madonna and Child* by Giotto described by Ghiberti, in the church of San Giorgio alla Costa in Florence and now in the Museo Diocesano di Santo Stefano al Ponte. The panel has been cut on both sides, but from what remains we can reconstruct the bright marble throne embellished with rose-colored moldings and strips of Cosmati work, terminating in a Gothic cusp edged with foliage-scrolls – exactly like those on the aedicules of the *Doctors of the Church* at Assisi. Here, too, small details, such as the rings and cord by which the cloth is suspended from the throne, are rendered with great clarity. In this painting we find the same deliberate contrast of fragility and strength, of

12. Madonna and Child, detail
Upper Church, Assisi

the delicately rendered minutiae of the supporting structure and the ponderous weight of the figures, that also characterizes the *Ognissanti Madonna*, now in the Uffizi. But let us return to Assisi, bearing in mind the image of the two elegant, slightly melancholy angels in the Florentine painting so that we can compare them with the figures in the Upper Church frescoes. Of particular interest is the angels' hairstyle, consisting of wide coils above the ears and loose waves at the back, which is exactly like that of the elderly Isaac.

The decoration of the Upper Church was planned from the very beginning to conclude with the *Legend of St. Francis* on the lower walls, which protrude slightly beyond the upper walls. The whole was conceived according to a scheme which incorporated both the iconographical and the decorative aspects of the frescoes. No representation in the Upper Church is duplicated, except for the *Crucifixion*, which appears among the scenes in the nave, and is repeated on either side on the east walls of the transept. In this case the repetition was intentional and must have been planned from the beginning, as is demonstrated by the fact that the two scenes appear in the same position in the Lower Church, where the aim of the old thirteenth-century decorations, destroyed when the side chapels were built, was to establish parallels between the life of Christ and that of St. Francis. This idea was repeated in the Upper Church with greater richness and with the inclusion of scenes from the Old Testament. At certain points the parallel becomes very evident; for instance, the *Confirmation of the Rule* appears below *Isaac Blessing Jacob*, and the *Death and Ascension of St. Francis* (who has just received the stigmata) below the *Crucifixion*.

13. Vault of the Doctors Upper Church, Assisi

14. Madonna and Child Museo Diocesano di Santo Stefano al Ponte, Florence

The *Legend of St. Francis* in the Upper Church at Assisi

A strong argument for the idea of a general plan for the whole nave is provided by the system of decoration, in which an impression of continuity is maintained in spite of the radical change in the pictorial conception which occurred over the course of the work. In fact, the decorative motif of the row of mock corbels which support the mock architrave at the top of the projecting wall where the *Legend of St. Francis* appears had already been used for the same purpose by Cimabue in his frescoes in the transept. This fact alone suggests that the decoration of the church, which was begun at a time when the basilica of San Francesco was perhaps the most important place of worship in Christendom – the center of the most widespread religious movement the West had known since the advent of Christianity – was carried out with few interruptions. And it might reasonably be supposed that the decoration of such an important church would not have been left incomplete for very long, nor the unsightly scaffolding employed in its decoration tolerated any longer than was necessary.

As for the part of the decoration carried out by Giotto, the motif of the mock corbels can be used as an indication of the order in which the *Scenes from the Old and New Testament* and the *Legend of St. Francis* were painted. We have already seen that Cimabue employed the same corbels in the frescoes in the transept, though his way of painting them was completely different from the manner in which Giotto was to use them above the St. Francis cycle. Cimabue's corbels are two-dimensional, and painted in inverted perspective, i.e. the side brackets are made to diverge – instead of converge, as they would appear to the eye – from the central one. The painted corbels above the *Legend of St. Francis* correspond much more to visual reality since they are represented as solid objects and converge towards the central corbel. The row of corbels on the ribs of the vault of

the *Doctors of the Church* was painted according to the system used by Cimabue, but in a small section of the upper walls, between *Joseph and His Brethren* and the *Pentecost* and between the *Resurrection* and the *Ascension*, the fake architecture is surmounted by a row of brackets painted by the same method Giotto was to use for the ones above the St. Francis cycle. This is evidently a method that he worked out gradually as the decoration proceeded.

There is another aspect to be considered. Work on the St. Francis cycle began with *St. Francis Giving His Mantle to a Poor Knight*, the second of the twenty-eight scenes, while the first scene, the *Homage of a Simple Man*, was probably painted last. This is because the beam of the iconostasis, or rood screen, a piece of which is still visible, was to be inserted into the wall in the area occupied by the first scene. Evidently, it was only towards the end of the work that it was decided to fresco the first and last areas of the wall as well, painting them in such a way that the beam could be inserted into the neutral area of the blue background.

There is a remarkable difference between the first and second scenes of the cycle. In the *Homage of a Simple Man* the painting has become softer, the transitions of color are more delicate and the clothing has a very soft, velvety consistency which, especially in the case of the figure on the far right, already looks forward to the Arena Chapel frescoes. But *St. Francis Giving His Mantle to a Poor Knight* is still distinguished by a transparent, almost metallic color which creates the effect of granite in the rocks of the landscape. Moreover, the head of the young St. Francis in this fresco is closer to those of Esau, Jacob, St. Gregory's acolyte, and the two mourners in the Santa Maria Novella *Crucifix* than it is to the softer, more mature head of the saint in the *Homage of a Simple Man*. In short, there would appear to be less differ-

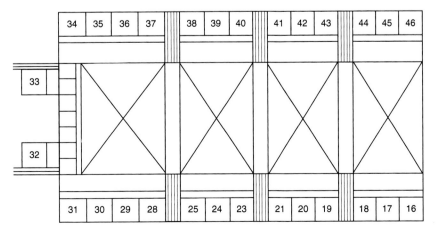

15. Interior of the Upper Church at Assisi

ence between Giotto's frescoes on the upper walls and the early works of the St. Francis cycle than there is between the first and last frescoes of the St. Francis cycle. This suggests that as soon as they had finished the frescoes on the upper walls, Giotto and his team of painters began work on the *Legend of St. Francis*, taking more time over it because there was a larger surface to cover, and because the work, being nearer the observer, had to be carried out with greater care.

The execution of large parts of the twenty-eight scenes of the *Legend of St. Francis*, especially the final ones, (for instance, the kneeling friars in the *Confirmation, St. Francis before the Sultan*, some of the figures in the *Institution of the Crib at Grec-* cio) is doubtless of a somewhat lower standard than one would expect from Giotto himself. But even though the contributions made by his assistants are sometimes so individual in their treatment that we can attempt to identify the individual artists (Memmo di Filippuccio? The Master of the Montefalco Crucifix? The Master of St. Cecilia? Marino da Perugia?), all the scenes, including the final ones, are distinguished by a unity of conception and a consistency of outlook found only in the work of Giotto. In fact, the works executed by these artists independently reveal that they never approached Giotto's level of achievement; the style of one painter is insufficiently articulated, another is over-expressive, yet another is excessively

16-18. Legend of St. Francis: Homage of a Simple Man; St. Francis Giving His Mantle to a Poor Knight; Dream of the Palace Filled with Weapons

concerned with detail. Only one work bears comparison with these frescoes: the *St. Francis Receiving the Stigmata* in the Louvre. And it is signed by Giotto.

I have already dealt with the mock architectural framework, so beautifully depicted in its detail, surrounding the *Legend of St. Francis*. Each bay is divided into three almost square panels, save for the bay nearest to the entrance, which has four compartments, and the facade wall, which has two sections higher than they are wide. The vanishing points are located in the center of each bay, as is indicated by the disposition of the painted corbels. This, the most extensive of all St. Francis cycles, and one which was to serve as a model for many years, consists of twenty-eight stories based on the official biography of the saint, St. Bonaventure's *Legenda Maior*. Each scene has an accompanying explanatory inscription in Latin.

The scene of *St. Francis Giving His Mantle to a Poor Knight*, the first to be painted, takes place in the open air, at the foot of two rocky hills. The town perched on the hill on the left is Assisi; we can see its crenelated walls, the profile of its towers and roofs against the sky and the church of San Damiano outside the walls. Anyone who has had the opportunity to see hillside towns such as Cortona, Spello and Assisi from the plain below can fully understand the accuracy of this painting. A rocky landscape like the one shown here, a legacy of Byzantine painting, may have first appeared in *Joseph Cast into the Pit by His Brothers* (as far as we can tell from what remains) or, more likely, in the *Death of Abel*, which has al-

most completely disappeared. It is a conception that was to be beautifully expressed in the *Miracle of the Spring* and *St. Francis Receiving the Stigmata* and adopted by nearly all painters up to the beginning of the fifteenth century. It was codified in the celebrated passage in Cennino Cennini's *Trattato della Pittura*, doubtless inspired by Giotto's principles: "If you want to paint natural-looking mountains, take some large jagged rocks, and paint them from nature, adding light and shade as reason dictates."

The beautifully rendered cloak in *St. Francis Giving His Mantle to a Poor Knight* is reminiscent of the blanket that covers the old patriarch's legs in *Isaac Blessing Jacob*. The folds of this garment have such convincing thickness that it almost seems possible to insert a hand into them. In the next scene, the *Dream of the Palace*, the blanket that covers St. Francis as he sleeps has a similar tangibility. The composition of this scene is very similar to that of the third fresco in the next bay, the *Dream of Innocent III*. The bedchambers in the two frescoes call to mind the scenes of Isaac, though the furnishings and architecture appear to be more in keeping with the style of Giotto's time. The two dreams are depicted very literally: the first dream is of a strange and narrow palace in the Italian Gothic style, which stands next to the bed as if it formed part of the chamber's sumptuous furnishings; the second is that of Innocent III. In his dream the pope saw the Church upheld by the Franciscans. The painter showed St. Francis literally propping up the church of San Giovanni in Laterano as it appeared at that date, after Nicholas IV's restoration of 1290. The facial expression of the youthful St. Francis as he supports the church is one of the most intense in the whole cycle.

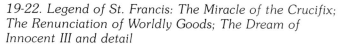

19-22. Legend of St. Francis: The Miracle of the Crucifix; The Renunciation of Worldly Goods; The Dream of Innocent III and detail

As if they were intended to emphasize the personal and private nature of the saint's early life, these first scenes are very simple, and contain few figures. This is especially evident in the *Miracle of the Crucifix*, where there are only two basic elements, the dilapidated church – where we can see the crucifix on the altar – and the young St. Francis. The church, set at an oblique angle, is shown with segments of the wall removed (like a broken vase) both to symbolize its state of moral decay and to enable us to see the inte-

rior with the speaking crucifix. St. Francis is there symbolically rather than actually, painted on a larger scale than the building.

This treatment of figure and architecture as independent elements was to remain a feature of fourteenth-century painting, becoming accentuated in the early fifteenth century, and employed in a deliberately unnatural way in certain late Gothic works. This trait can also be seen in the painters of the Early Netherlandish School; Jan van Eyck's *Virgin in a Church*, in which the Virgin's head is on a level with the capitals in the nave, is a typical example, and one that can be compared to the *Miracle of the Crucifix*. The conception of a pictorial story as an agglomeration of separate incidents was to be greatly simplified in Giotto's later works, especially in the frescoes in the Bardi and Peruzzi Chapels in Santa Croce. But it took the rationalism of Brunelleschi, and the art of Donatello and Masaccio, to do away with it completely.

The next scene gives us an opportunity to examine one of the most important of Giotto's innovations. Although the mastery of the method of representing the third dimension is of fundamental importance, there are other innovations which are no less significant to the development of Western painting. Among these must be included the use of eloquent gesture, the communication of strong emotions through attitude and facial expression. In the *Renunciation of Worldly Goods*, St. Francis's father ex-

18

23-26. Legend of St. Francis: The Confirmation of
the Rule and detail; The Vision of the Flaming Chariot;
The Vision of the Thrones

presses his anger in his grimace, in his gesture of lifting the hem of his gown (as if he were about to dash at his son), and in his clenched fist; the effect is heightened by the gesture of his friend, who holds him back by the arm. Within the limits of the dignity and self-restraint that Giotto impresses on all his characters, the father's anger is expressed clearly and vividly.

St. Francis Preaching before Honorius III is one of the scenes of the *Legend of St. Francis* in which

gesture, attitude and facial expression are essential to the story, and in this respect it was to become a model for fourteenth-century painters. Although some have felt St. Francis's gesture to be vulgar, it was certainly not considered coarse in Giotto's day: that lively way of indicating with the thumb was to reappear in such paintings as Pietro Lorenzetti's *Virgin with St. Francis and St. John* in the Lower Church of San Francesco. The prelates' gestures of meditation and wonder were to become extremely common in the course of the fourteenth century, but here they were total innovations.

Of the frescoes on the upper walls, it is the *Lamentation* which provides a rich display of profoundly expressive gestures of sorrow. This scene was usually depicted with the mourners screaming and thronging around the dead Christ, but here it becomes a masterly interpretation of grief reminiscent of the attitudes of classical statuary. The tone is livelier and less rhetorical in the scenes of sorrow of the St. Francis cycle – the *Death of the Knight of Celano,* the *Death and Ascension of St. Francis,* and *St. Francis Mourned by St. Clare.* It should be remembered, however, that the *Legend of St. Francis* tells the story of a man who had died within living memory and deals with events that were almost contemporary, and with men and women who lacked the legendary glory of Old and New Testament figures. There can be no doubt that the tone of the frescoes

27-31. Legend of St. Francis: Expulsion of the Devils from Arezzo; The Ordeal by Fire before the Sultan and detail; The Ecstasy of St. Francis; Institution of the Crib at Greccio

on the upper walls is more courtly and more solemn, as it was to be in the frescoes depicting the lives of the Virgin and Christ in the Arena Chapel at Padua, while in the *Legend of St. Francis* the narrative tone is livelier and more direct to suit the characters.

At that time Dante was theorizing about various styles: a "superior" style for tragedy, an "inferior" style for comedy (his *Divine Comedy*), and a style "of compassion" (*miserorum*) for elegy. The three styles had their respective idioms in an "illustrious vernacular," a "vernacular sometimes mediocre, sometimes humble," and an "exclusively humble vernacular." And when Jacopo Torriti included St. Francis and St. Anthony of Padua among the time-honored saints of the Gospels in his apse mosaics in San Giovanni in Laterano and Santa Maria Maggiore, in Rome, he made them on a smaller scale than the others. Thus a lesser dignity was conferred on these new saints,

who were felt to be intruders in such a solemn gathering. Boniface VIII even planned to have them removed from the apse of San Giovanni in Laterano.

However unsatisfactory the execution of the figures may be, the *Confirmation of the Rule* and *St. Francis Preaching before Honorius III* have the most organic spatial constructions of all the Upper Church frescoes. These scenes, which have a perfectly centralized viewpoint, are two of the most outstanding examples of Giotto's conception of space as a cubic box that is open at the front. Notice how cleverly this space has been contrived. Our attention appears to be drawn to the upper part of each fresco, occupied by a series of protruding arches supported by sturdy consoles in the *Confirmation of the Rule*, and by the first surviving depiction of a groin vault in the history of Italian painting in *St. Francis Preaching before Honorius III*. Such perfection of spatial construction is found only in the frescoes in the Arena Chapel, Padua, and the Bardi Chapel in Santa Croce, and those in the right transept of the Lower Church at Assisi, all of which are by Giotto.

Another noteworthy feature of the *Confirmation of the Rule* is the arrangement in depth of rows of kneeling friars behind St. Francis. The first time anything of the kind appears in Italian painting is in the scene of *Joseph and His Brethren* on the upper wall, where Joseph's brothers are always painted in horizontal rows parallel to the picture plane, as if they were standing on a series of progressively higher stools. Duccio still preferred this arrangement for the saints in his *Maestà* at Siena, while Simone Martini showed the rows of figures around the Virgin at a slightly oblique angle in his *Maestà* in the Palazzo Pubblico, Siena. The latter system had been introduced and systematically employed by Giotto, in perfect harmony with his conception of pictorial space.

The five scenes from the *Vision of the Flaming Chariot* to *St. Francis in Ecstasy* are characterized by inferior workmanship, especially in the figures, though they do contain some remarkable inventions. The conception of the sleeping friars in the *Vision of the Flaming Chariot* is extraordinary; one of them is a more expressionistic version of the foreshortened soldier who sleeps with his head resting on the back of his hand in the upper-wall scene of the *Resurrection*. Worthy of note in the *Vision of the Thrones* are the *trompe-l'œil* clarity of the thrones suspended in space and the representation of the lamp in front of the altar, which has a cord for lowering it to replenish the oil. The *Expulsion of the Devils from Arezzo* is impressive for its depiction of a walled city, which is shown as a vertical mass of houses, towers, chimneys, roofs and roof terraces, all perceived as components of a single entity. The large church on the left, seen from the end with the apse, bears a strong resemblance to the parish church of Santa Maria in Arezzo.

In many respects the *Institution of the Crib at Greccio* is one of the most interesting scenes in the cycle. It is set inside the church, viewed from the presbytery, in front of the transept dividing the latter from the nave. As women were not allowed in the presbytery, they are shown looking on from the doorway of the transept. Everything in the church is seen from behind: the pulpit with its lighted candles; the table of the lectern, on which is placed the antiphonary, or book of responses, of the four singing friars; the tabernacle in the style of Arnolfo di Cambio, decorated with Christmas garlands above the altar; and the cross, which leans towards the nave, its wooden backing and supporting structure clearly visible, something that was unheard-of at the time. In this scene too, many of the figures have been executed somewhat mechanically by Giotto's assistants (especially the heads of the priest and the acolytes standing behind him on the right), though the highly expressive, lifelike figures of the singing friars are among the best in the whole of the St. Francis cycle.

The two scenes on the entrance wall, the *Miracle of the Spring* and the *Preaching to the Birds*, the

32, 33. Legend of St. Francis: Miracle of the Spring; Preaching to the Birds

34-37. Legend of St. Francis: Death of the Knight of Celano; St. Francis Preaching before Honorius III; The Apparition in the Chapter House at Arles; St. Francis Receiving the Stigmata

compositions in which Giotto's hand is most apparent, are too famous to require a lengthy description. As Giotto's conception of the landscape in the former has already been mentioned, I shall merely point out the amazing precision with which the ass's packsaddle has been rendered. The *Preaching to the Birds*, on the other side of the doorway, provides an obvious foil for the *Miracle of the Spring*. The former is set on an open plain, where the figures are overshadowed by tall trees, while the vegetation in the latter consists of the wild scrub of the Mediterranean region, which must have been typical of the uncultivated uplands in Giotto's day.

Between these scenes, above the entrance, Giotto frescoed a large tondo of the *Virgin and Child* and two smaller tondi of angels. Although in a very poor state, these images are among the finest in the Upper Church, especially for the way in which the figure of the Virgin spreads out like a dome, the vividness of her veil and the sturdy grip of her left hand. In the Child we see the first smile in Italian painting.

26

The four scenes in the first bay of the left wall deal with the last events in the saint's life, and are among the most fascinating in the cycle. Some of them have already been described, so it will be enough to point out the table in the *Death of the Knight of Celano*, which is covered with a lovely embroidered tablecloth and laid with food, crockery and cutlery. Worthy of notice in *St. Francis Preaching before Honorius III* is the rich Cosmati work on the pope's foot stool, whose bright colors recall the vault of the *Doctors*. In the *Apparition at Arles* we are given a remarkable oblique view of the chapterhouse, its back wall pierced by three openings. The massive figures of the friars seen from behind anticipate certain features of the Paduan *Lamentation*. The range of attitudes adopted by the friars, the varied colors of their habits and the massive figure of St. Anthony on the left are among the most memorable aspects of this work. In the *St. Francis Receiving the Stigmata*, the rocks take on an almost phosphorescent luminosity on what is the darkest wall in the church.

Giotto's authorship of some parts of the following frescoes is often questioned, and in the case of those in the last bay, denied completely. The fact that a work was painted by the artist himself mattered much less to the public of Giotto's day than it does to us, accustomed as we are to assigning importance (and therefore a price) only to pictures, preferably signed, by an individual artist. In those days the artist worked with a team of assistants, and not every painting that left his studio was entirely his own work, even though it might have been signed by him. If the St. Francis cycle at Assisi had borne a signature it would probably have been Giotto's, however likely it was that his assistants played a key role in the execution.

The final frescoes have a greater affinity with the overall cycle than with the works of other painters who have been suggested as Giotto's assistants. Even the last three scenes have very little relation to the

38-40. Legend of St. Francis: Death of St. Francis, The Appearance to Brother Agostino and the Bishop of Assisi; Verification of the Stigmata

41-43. Legend of St. Francis: St. Francis Mourned by St. Clare; Canonization of St. Francis; The Dream of Gregory IX

meticulously Gothic manner used by the Master of St. Cecilia in the painting, now in the Uffizi, from which he takes his name. They have much more in common with the other frescoes of the St. Francis cycle, a fact we can more readily acknowledge if we admit that some development was inevitable over the course of the execution of such a complex work.

No one can deny the superb quality of certain parts of the frescoes in the second bay of the left wall, such as the beautiful angels flanking the ones bearing the saint's soul to paradise in the *Death and Ascen-*

sion of St. Francis. The setting of the *Verification of the Stigmata* inside the church, where the three icons – the *Virgin*, *Christ Crucified* and *St. Michael* – on the rood screen are shown leaning forward, and the curved wall of the apse is shown in the background, is a conception found only in the *Institution of the Crib at Greccio*. In *St. Francis Mourned by St. Clare* the facade of an Italian Gothic church is shown in the background, the first representation of its kind, decorated not only with marble and Cosmati work but also with sculpture in high relief.

This and the next scene, the *Canonization of St. Francis*, in which, despite its damaged condition, we can still perceive the splendid arrangement of the group of onlookers, lead naturally to a consideration of the style of dress Giotto adopted for his lay figures, both male and female – a consideration which can also be extended to other scenes such as the *Homage of a Simple Man* and the *Renunciation of Worldly Goods*. He evidently thought it incongruous to use, as the Berlinghieri had done, the semi-classical dress customarily used in Biblical scenes to represent events from the very recent past. So he dressed his lay figures in contemporary clothing, just as he had made the buildings in the scenes reflect the architecture of his own time. This idea was so successful that it inspired artists over the next two centuries to introduce figures in modern dress into their works, even when representing events from the past. In considering the stylistic differences between the upper wall frescoes and the *Legend of St. Francis* (or the latter and the Paduan frescoes), we should bear in mind the realistic effect created by the use of contemporary dress.

Giotto was not the first to use modern dress: an anonymous artist had already done so in the painting of *St. Clare*, dated 1283, in the church of the same name at Assisi. In this painting the lay figures in the small lateral scenes are dressed in what is unmistakably contemporary clothing. This style of dress, in many respects similar to that of the lay figures in the St. Francis cycle, appears antiquated in comparison to the style of clothing depicted in the Arena Chapel frescoes. We must therefore conclude that the Assisi frescoes were painted much earlier than the Paduan ones.

The *Dream of Gregory IX* is distinguished by yet another remarkable representation of space. The scene is set in a well-proportioned room akin to those in the *Confirmation of the Rule* and *St. Francis Preaching before Honorius III*. However, the fact that the spatial construction is no longer perfectly centralized constitutes a step towards the artist's later treatment of interiors. Of special interest here is the strong definition of the curtain suspended from the ceiling, which heightens the credibility of the spatial setting.

The final scenes of the story – the *Healing of the Man from Lerida*, the *Confession of the Woman from Benevento*, and the *Liberation of the Repentant Heretic* – are characterized by an extremely delicate architectural structure, and slender, elongated

figures. Yet parts of these works are of very high quality, and comparable to the work of Giotto himself. This is true of the beautiful secondary episode of St. Francis kneeling before Christ in the upper left-hand corner of the *Confession of the Woman from Benevento*, and of the delicate, mock bas-reliefs on the round tower, inspired by Trajan's Column, on the right in the *Liberation of the Repentant Heretic*. Moreover, the figure of the prisoner, a man named Pietro d'Assisi, anticipates certain physical types which appear in the Arena Chapel frescoes – for instance, the bearded man kneeling on the far left in the *Prayer of the Suitors*.

The evolution towards the softer effects characteristic of the Paduan frescoes has already been men-

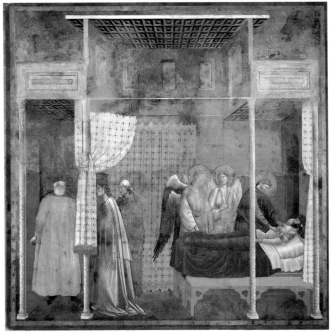

44-46. *Legend of St. Francis: The Healing of the Man from Lerida; The Confession of the Woman from Benevento; The Liberation of the Repentant Heretic*

tioned in connection with the *Homage of a Simple Man*, which is the first scene of the story, although the last to be executed. It has even been suggested that these final works were painted after the Arena Chapel frescoes, but all we have to do to exclude this possibility is to consider one detail – the profile. From a strictly naturalistic point of view the profiles in the St. Francis cycle, including the final scenes, appear to be imperfectly realized. By contrast, the profiles in the Paduan frescoes are wholly convincing and, moreover, they are used to create some of the most dramatic moments in the narrative, as can be seen in the *Betrayal of Christ*, where the profiles of Christ and Judas are juxtaposed in the center of the scene.

From the fourth century up until the end of the thirteenth, sacred and important figures were invariably shown frontally. As a result, the use of the profile, which was reserved for representations of evil or marginal figures, became less frequent as time passed. To indicate that one figure was addressing another, the artist would merely incline one head, still seen in full face, towards another. As a result of this convention, the ability of artists to "see" and represent the profile gradually diminished, as is demonstrated by the few works in which it was employed. The presence of this "defect," like that of the archaic form of the "angelic spirits," in the *Legend of St. Francis* provides further proof of the fact that the Assisi frescoes predate those in the Arena Chapel.

The Assisi frescoes would seem to belong to an early stage in Giotto's career, when he and his workshop were still attempting to assimilate the Gothic innovations which were invading the Italian visual arts. If this is true, then the delicacy of the architectural structures and the elongation of the figures in the final scenes of the St. Francis cycle may also justify suggestions that the Master of St. Cecilia worked on them. These Gothic elements, which also appear in the predella scenes of *St. Francis Receiving the Stig-*

47. *St. Francis Receiving the Stigmata*
314x162 cm
Louvre, Paris

48. *Badia Polyptych*
91x334 cm
Uffizi, Florence

mata in the Louvre, signed by Giotto, go back to the period in which Duccio di Buoninsegna was approaching the mature Gothic style of his late works. The great Sienese goldsmith Guccio di Mannaia, craftsman of the chalice donated by Nicholas IV to the Franciscan basilica between 1288 and 1292, was also an early exponent of the French Gothic style in central Italy.

If we consider the St. Francis cycle as a whole, we are forced to admit that Giotto's interpretation of the famous saint is not particularly mystical: St. Francis is a pious and devout figure, yet solid and earthly, far removed from the ascetic saint in earlier thirteenth-century paintings. The objects in these frescoes have been couched in such concrete form that even the metaphysical episodes seem to have been brought within the sphere of everyday experience.

The fact that this cycle served for so long as a model for the representation of the saint's life is probably due to the dominance of the more worldly interpretation of St. Francis's teaching by the "Conventual" faction in both the papacy and the Franciscan order itself. It was an interpretation particularly agreeable to the rich Roman Curia, and in keeping with the interests of the new middle class which had control of the main cities of central Italy.

The opposing faction in the order, known as the "Spirituals," wished to return to the simple, ascetic life of poverty demanded by St. Francis himself.

I have already touched upon the panel in the Louvre with *St. Francis Receiving the Stigmata*, signed by Giotto and painted for the church of San Francesco at Pisa. The main scene and the three smaller scenes of the predella – the *Dream of Innocent III*, the *Confirmation of the Rule*, and the *Preaching to the Birds* – are obvious variations on the theme of the Assisi frescoes. Critics have tended to concentrate on the unmistakable iconographical similarity of the two groups and pay less attention to their equally evident stylistic affinities. What is most interesting to note in this work is the refined Gothic elegance, apparent in the elongated figures of the predella scenes. The panel is stylistically close to the last Assisi scenes

and was the point of departure for the style of Florentine artists like the Master of St. Cecilia, although he never achieved the degree of spatial coherence shown by Giotto here. It is this signed work, even more than the remains of the *Navicella* mosaic, which constitutes the most important proof of Giotto's authorship of the Assisi frescoes.

The *Badia Polyptych* (Uffizi, Florence), which was mentioned by Ghiberti and discovered some time ago in the church of Santa Croce, must have been painted around the same time. In spite of the very poor condition of the work, we can still clearly perceive the solemnity of treatment which Giotto reserved for these saints. The dignified row of the half-length figures in the five panels and the rhythmical repetition of the nameplate on the gold ground above their heads make this work one of the artist's masterpieces. The Virgin recalls the one in the tondo above the entrance of the Upper Church at Assisi.

Giotto's stay in Rimini, which was recorded by contemporary chroniclers, must have preceded the decoration of the Arena Chapel at Padua. The precocious flowering of a Rimini school of painting clearly inspired by his art bears this out, as does the fact that the Rimini school appears to reflect a stage in Giotto's development still fairly closely tied to the criteria of simple contiguity used to link the architectural settings of many of the frescoes in Assisi, something which appears to have been superseded in the Scrovegni Chapel.

Direct evidence that he worked at Rimini is provided by the *Crucifix* in the Tempio Malatestiano in Rimini, which has unfortunately lost the panels once attached to the arms and apex (one of these, a painting of *God the Father*, has been found in a private collection in England). It is a nobler version of the Santa Maria Novella *Crucifix*, already showing signs of the artist's mature treatment of the subject. However, its pronounced plastic emphasis and definition of the features link it to somewhat earlier works, such as the *Badia Polyptych* and the *St. Francis Receiving the Stigmata* in the Louvre.

49. Crucifix
428x299 cm
Tempio Malatestiano, Rimini

The Arena Chapel at Padua

The fresco decorations in the Arena Chapel at Padua have long been considered the greatest of Giotto's work and one of the major turning points in the history of European painting. He was probably about forty years old when he began work on the chapel.

His Paduan patron, Enrico Scrovegni, was a wealthy, politically ambitious merchant who in 1300 had acquired the ruins of the old Roman arena at Padua as a site for his house and adjoining chapel. Although existing documents are somewhat vague on the subject, it seems that the chapel was built, decorated and consecrated between 1303 and 1305. The date of the frescoes is not certain and is variously placed between 1304 and 1312-13, although a date of about 1305 appears the most acceptable to this author.

A fairly compelling argument is provided by the indications, not very numerous but precise, that come to us from the style of the clothing: judging by these, the frescoes in Padua predate a polyptych painted by Giuliano da Rimini in 1307, now in the Gardner Museum at Boston.

Owing to the small size of the chapel, illuminated by six windows on the right wall, Giotto had at his disposal a wall space that was both restricted and asymmetrical. In order to carry out the extensive iconographical scheme, he took the areas between the windows as his point of departure, planning to depict two scenes one above the other in each of these. Using this as the basic unit of measure, he divided up the walls of the chapel into panels.

Here too the system of frames used to separate the scenes sets out to create the illusion that it is the architectural structure of the church's own walls. Certainly, it is a less conspicuous framework than in Assisi, but clearly visible nonetheless. Besides, the situation was different: here a series of images had be to arranged on four different levels, whereas the scenes in San Francesco were laid out horizontally on a single level.

The scenes on the walls are arranged in four tiers, and are surrounded by a structure that seems to form part of the architecture of the chapel. However, the framing is less accentuated than in the *Legend of St. Francis*, on just one level, since exaggerated projections would have been unsuited to the modest proportions of the Paduan chapel. Furthermore, the simulated projections of the Assisi framework had been suggested by the real projection of the lower walls, whereas the walls of the Arena Chapel are perfectly flat. The scenes are separated vertically by wide bands of mock marble which are richly decorated with Cosmati work and interspersed with small, lobed panels containing representations of minor figures.

A significant innovation is the dado painted to imitate veined marble and topped by a slightly projecting cornice, which, as at Assisi, is supported by a row of tiny corbels. Between the mock marble panels are small monochrome frescoes imitating sculptural reliefs, representing the *Seven Virtues* and *Seven Vices*. These were also carved on Giotto's Campanile. The simulated monochrome reliefs gave rise to a kind of fresco decoration that was to flourish in the fifteenth and sixteenth centuries (the most famous examples are the frescoes by Paolo Uccello in the Green Cloister of Santa Maria Novella and the ones by Andrea del Sarto in the cloister of the Scalzo, both in Florence). A parallel development can be seen in the imitation statues that Flemish painters included in the side panels of their altarpieces, beginning with Jan van Eyck's polyptych of the *Adoration of the Lamb*.

An illusionism even more daring than that at Assisi is found in the frescoes flanking the chancel arch, just above the dado. Instead of "stories," Giotto painted two views of the interiors of what appear to be sacristies or a choir, in perfect perspective. The effect is

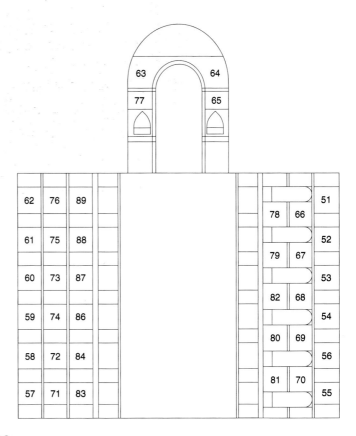

50. View of the Arena Chapel

34

so realistic that we feel we are looking into actual rooms. Our gaze moves beyond the pointed arch to the groin vault of each room, and thence to the Gothic mullioned window. In front of the window a lamp hangs from the ceiling by a rope, with a small ring at the end used to raise and lower it (as in the *Vision of the Thrones*). The sky visible through the window is not the abstract blue of the background of the frescoes, but a much lighter shade clearly intended to represent the real sky, something quite exceptional for its time. That the two symmetrical chapels appear to have approximately the same vanishing point is an astonishing anticipation of fifteenth-century perspective. Though their significance was once ignored, these small scenes are now recognized as an extremely important phase in the development of Giotto's conception of pictorial space.

Since the chapel is relatively small, and the right hand wall is interrupted by the windows, Giotto had to divide the wall surface into smaller panels than those at Assisi (the Paduan frescoes measure 200 x 185 cm, those at Assisi 270 x 230 cm). This explains the different dimensions of the figures in relation to the panels and to the space that encloses them, since the figures in a fresco had to be as close as possible to life size. It is also one of the reasons the Paduan frescoes acquired the extraordinary sense of concentration and pictorial unity that is so appreciated today, and a possible explanation for the unusually stocky proportions of the figures.

Compared with the Assisi frescoes, the painting has grown softer; the subtler modeling gives the figures and objects a greater volume. All harshness has been eliminated. The figures' gestures maintain an

51, 52. Scenes from the Life of Joachim: The Expulsion of Joachim from the Temple; Joachim among the Shepherds

53-55. Scenes from the Life of Joachim: Annunciation of the Angel to St. Anne; The Sacrifice of Joachim; The Meeting at the Golden Gate

56. Scenes from the Life of Joachim: The Dream of Joachim, detail

equilibrium between the *gravitas* of antiquity and the grace of French Gothic art. The narrative tone is solemn and elevated, yet relaxed and serene. The most important and dignified figures have a majestic air, an expression of conviction and a profound, concentrated gaze, yet they are warm and reassuringly human.

However, the scenes are not made up exclusively of prominent characters; there is a supporting cast of minor ones whose lesser dignity is invariably emphasized by the expressiveness of their features and live-

57. Scenes from the Life of Mary: The Birth of the Virgin

liness of their attitudes (as well as their style of dress). We need only observe the faces of the servants waiting to pour the wine in the *Marriage at Cana*; or of Christ's tormenters in the scenes of the Passion, which are close to caricatures; or the smiles of St. Anne's companions in the *Meeting at the Golden Gate*, or the bustling midwives in the *Birth of the Virgin*.

This more prosaic tone characterizes the personifications of the virtues and vices, in which the more mundane atmosphere is accentuated by the use of contemporary dress. In this respect the *Virtues* and

Vices bear the same relation to the other frescoes in the chapel as the *Legend of St. Francis* does to the frescoes on the upper walls of the Upper Church. It is no mere coincidence that the extent of Giotto's intervention in the *Virtues* and *Vices* has also been the subject of controversy, while the sublime tone of the scenes from the lives of Mary and Christ has often led critics to overlook the weakness of certain parts, such as some of the marginal figures in the frescoes in the upper rows (for instance, the three figures on the far right and the shepherd on the left in the *Meeting at the Golden Gate*, clearly executed by his less skilful assistants).

38

Let us now take a closer look at the frescoes, following the sequence of the narrative and pausing to examine some of them in detail. We begin with the six scenes of Joachim and Anne in the top row on the right wall. They tell of how Joachim was expelled from the temple because of his childlessness, how he took refuge among the shepherds in the mountains, how the angel appeared to Anne with the news that she would bear a child, how Joachim made a sacrificial offering that was favorably received by God and how the angel appeared to him in a dream to tell him of the coming birth of Mary. The series concludes with Joachim's return to Jerusalem, where he meets his wife Anne at the Golden Gate and Mary is conceived in the kiss that Anne bestows on her elderly husband. This is a story with a happy ending, and the scene has a quiet, pastoral atmosphere suggested by the rocky landscape and the shepherds with their sheep, whose soft, lifelike fleece has been meticulously rendered.

If we compare these scenes with the Assisi frescoes, we notice that here the space is more confined, the figures take up more room and the architectural settings have been limited to a single structure in almost every scene, necessary for the telling of the story. Although all the scenes have their memorable aspects, one in particular, the *Annunciation to St. Anne*, is well worth examining in detail.

St. Anne's house consists of a bare framework that is intended to indicate an actual dwelling. It has been given the same concreteness as the buildings in the Assisi frescoes, but since it is the only one in the scene it acquires greater prominence and clarity. It is a symbolic house, and as such decidedly small for its inhabitants, as is demonstrated by the tiny window. But it is just this lack of room that underlines its con-

58-60. Scenes from the Life of Mary: The Presentation of the Virgin in the Temple; The Rods Brought to the Temple; The Prayer of the Suitors

creteness and depth. The interior and furnishings of Anne's room are so beautifully depicted that their only counterparts are the ones in some of the Assisi frescoes. The sole witness to the event is the servant, who sits out on the porch, spinning; the skirt of her dress is stretched between her knees, creating deep folds that heighten the solidity of her form. Her dress has the same tangibility as the cloak given away by St. Francis in one of the scenes at Assisi, though it has been modified by a softer, thicker application of paint.

The following six scenes on the opposite wall show the *Birth of the Virgin*, the *Presentation of*

61, 62. *Scenes from the Life of Mary: The Marriage of the Virgin; The Wedding Procession*

the Virgin in the Temple and the four episodes pertaining to her marriage: the *Rods Brought to the Temple*, the *Prayer of the Suitors*, the *Marriage of the Virgin* and the *Wedding Procession*. This series also remains faithful to the principle of the single architectural structure. St. Anne's house in the *Birth of the Virgin* is a repetition of the one in the *Annunciation to St. Anne*. The *Presentation of the Virgin* takes place in the same building as the one in the scene of the *Expulsion of Joachim from the Temple*, but viewed from the opposite side. The temple in the *Marriage of the Virgin* appears three times in the series. The kneeling figures in the *Prayer of the Suitors* are seen from the side or from behind, and display that massiveness so typical of Giotto's Paduan

63, 64. Scenes from the Life of Mary: Annunciation

period, an effect obtained by simplifying the drapery and anatomy to such an extent that the bodies appear to be perfectly solid.

The lunette above the chancel arch and the areas on either side of it, the most conspicuous wall surface in the chapel, is occupied by the *Annunciation*, the event to which the chapel was dedicated. In the upper section *God the Father Enthroned* is painted on a poorly preserved panel which also serves as a door. The striking mosaic decorations on the steps of the throne, which are painted in fresco, call to mind the Assisi frescoes, especially the *Doctors of the Church*. The group of angels round the throne is so skillfully arranged that we are given the impression that even Heaven has depth. They calmly move about, play their instruments, sing and take each other by the hand as if they were about to dance. This extraordinary conception anticipates the solutions adopted by Fra Angelico's for his images of Paradise by more than a century, while the small angels playing wind instruments at the ends call to mind the ones that make up the procession in Nanni di Banco's relief of the *Assumption of the Virgin* above the Porta della Mandorla in Florence Cathedral, also executed more than a century after the frescoes in the Scrovegni Chapel.

The *Annunciation* takes place in the lower section of the fresco, in the two spandrels flanking the chancel arch. Each of the two protagonists, Gabriel and Mary, kneels within a shrine which has been set at an angle to suggest that it faces the other; for this reason we see only the exteriors and a small part of the interiors of the two structures. Of all the buildings

in the Paduan frescoes, these shrines are most reminiscent of the architectural settings at Assisi, because of the curtains and the complicated consoles supporting the balconies. The self-possessed figures of Gabriel and Mary, especially the latter, have been given an extraordinary solidity. The foreshortening of Mary's arms has been carried out with a precision that anticipates the technical accomplishments of the fifteenth century.

The illusion of depth in these scenes is heightened by another of Giotto's innovations which appears throughout the chapel. Although by this time he had mastered the technique of representing figures in profile, he was left with the problem of how to represent their haloes, since the halo of a figure seen frontally appears as a solid disk attached behind the head, whereas that of a figure in profile should, logically, appear foreshortened. He attempted to solve the problem by making the haloes of figures in profile oval, like those of Gabriel and Mary in this scene. Later he was to abandon this solution, but it should certainly be seen as part of his research into space and one of the problems that he was continually tackling in his effort to represent three-dimensional reality on a two-dimensional surface.

The narrative continues with the scene of the *Visitation*, which appears in the panel directly below the Virgin of the *Annunciation*, on the right-hand side of the chancel arch. Here the figures are more conspicuous since they are painted to the same scale as those of the other frescoes, though the area itself is quite small. The five scenes on the right wall represent the *Nativity*, the *Adoration of the Magi*, the *Presentation in the Temple*, the *Flight into Egypt*, and the *Slaughter of the Innocents*. The well-constructed shed in the first scene reappears in the second, set at a slightly different angle. The temple in the third scene is the same one that appears in the *Expulsion of Joachim from the Temple* and the *Presentation of the Virgin in the Temple*, but this time we are shown only the shrine over the altar.

The *Flight into Egypt*, one of the most famous of the Arena Chapel frescoes, is set in a rocky landscape like the one in *St. Francis Receiving the Stigmata* at Assisi, although it is softer in appearance. Mary and her child form an isolated group in the center of the scene, their solemnity enhanced by the rich, beautiful-

65. *Scenes from the Life of Mary: Visitation and the "choir" underneath*

ly rendered folds of her cloak. Her profile is much more convincing than any of those in the frescoes at Assisi, a sign that once the artist had freed himself from the medieval prejudice against the profile he lost no time in mastering it. We can only imagine the startling effect this Virgin in full profile must have had on Giotto's contemporaries, accustomed as they were to the pictorial conventions still respected by other painters.

The *Slaughter of the Innocents* is the only scene in the chapel in which two buildings appear. The octagonal structure on the right recalls a baptistery (an allusion to the baptism of blood of the unfortunate infants?), and is depicted with even greater clarity than the structures at Assisi. One feels that it is a real building, an effect that is heightened by the subtle distinction made between the walls of the radial chapels and the buttresses that divide them; by the moldings of green marble; by the sky visible through the mullioned windows, which suggests that the alternation of buttress and chapel continues beyond our view; and by the interplay of light and shade. Giotto's handling of the shadows in this scene (note the shadow under the roof of Herod's balcony) is even more skilful than in his Assisi frescoes, and provides yet another demonstration of the realism of his art. There are no sacred figures in this scene, and the center of the composition has been reserved for the figure of an executioner, who is drawing his sword to kill a child still clinging to its mother's breast. His attitude is echoed in the figure behind him, Herculean and ominous under his hood.

The six scenes on the opposite wall – *Christ among the Doctors*, the *Baptism of Christ*, the *Marriage at Cana*, the *Raising of Lazarus*, the *Entry into Jerusalem*, and the *Expulsion of the Moneychangers from the Temple* – have the most solemn narrative tone of all the frescoes, perhaps because they deal with Christ's adult mission.

Christ among the Doctors is the most poorly preserved of all the frescoes in the chapel, but we can still make out its splendid architectural setting. It was the first of the Paduan frescoes to be set wholly within an interior and was laid out according to a scheme which recalls scenes in Assisi like the *Confirmation of the Rule* and *St. Francis Preaching before Honorius III*. It is even more reminiscent of the *Apparition to Gregory IX*, which has the same, slightly off-center viewpoint. In both cases this was determined by the position of the fresco, the Assisi scene being at the end of its bay and the Paduan scene next to the entrance, at the far end of the left wall of the chapel.

The very high quality of parts of the *Baptism of Christ* becomes evident if we consider the awe-inspiring face of Christ, the skilful foreshortening of God the Father and the masterly execution of the

66. Scenes from the Life of Christ: Nativity

heads of John the Baptist and the two disciples behind him. However, the water in which Christ stands
is painted in a completely irrational manner, since if it
rises to his navel it should cover part of the rocks and
at least the feet of the other figures. This strange river has its origins in a deeply rooted iconographical
convention which could be considered emblematic of
the medieval artist's inability to "see" the reality of

this world (or, if we prefer, of his desire to render that
reality abstract). We do not know if this inconsistency
is a result of an oversight on the part of the artist, if
it was imposed on him by his patron or if it represents
a surrender to iconographic tradition in order to avoid
showing Christ completely nude. At all events, it
demonstrates that Giotto was still capable of being influenced by the conventions of medieval painting.

The dramatic tension of the two preceding scenes
is temporarily relieved in the *Marriage at Cana*,

67-69. Scenes from the Life of Christ: The Adoration of the Magi; The Presentation in the Temple; The Flight into Egypt

44

70-73. *Scenes from the Life of Christ: Slaughter of the Innocents; Christ among the Doctors; Baptism of Christ; The Raising of Lazarus*

where the homeliness of the interior is emphasized by the striped wall hanging, the round-bellied amphorae and the comic characterization of the guests and servants. The tone becomes solemn again in the three scenes that follow, but even here Giotto never misses an opportunity for heightening the realism of such things as the wooden cages and stalls in the *Expulsion of the Moneychangers from the Temple*. The cage held by one of the moneychangers was an afterthought, added when the plaster was almost dry and for this reason barely visible today. We now come to the scene on the left side of the chancel arch, *Judas Receiving Payment for His Betrayal*. Judas is shown in profile, with a black halo and with the devil standing behind him. His portrayal is in keeping with those simple didactic precepts that would have evil revealed by an ugly face.

The story continues in the row below, on the window side of the chapel. Here we have a symmetrical arrangement of scenes (an outdoor scene flanked by two indoor scenes) from the Passion of Christ – the *Last Supper*, the *Washing of Feet*, the *Kiss of Judas*, *Christ before Caiaphas*, and the *Flagellation*. The quiet solemnity of the first two scenes, which have been given the same setting, is followed by the frenzied activity in the *Kiss of Judas*, where the scene is dominated by the massive figure of Judas, one of the most impressive of Giotto's creations, and the

46

74. Scenes from the Life of Christ: The Marriage at Cana

sweep of his cloak as he reaches out to embrace Christ. The proximity of the beautiful profile of Christ and the repellent one of Judas becomes a confrontation of absolute good and absolute evil. The scene of *Christ before Caiaphas* provides yet another demonstration of the artist's increasing independence from the pictorial conventions of his day. This is a night scene in which a torch, now darkened because of alterations in the pigment, illuminates the wooden ceiling from beneath, an effect of unprecedented subtlety in a period when most artists continued to adhere

to the anti-naturalistic canons of medieval painting.

In the corresponding tier on the opposite wall are the *Road to Calvary*, the *Crucifixion*, the *Lamentation*, the Resurrection represented by the *Noli me tangere* scene (instead of the three Marys at the tomb), the *Ascension*, and the *Pentecost*. Apart from the *Road to Calvary*, these scenes all appear on the upper walls of the Upper Church at Assisi.

The *Road to Calvary*, which, like the scene above it, *Christ among the Doctors*, is in very poor condition, shows the procession to Calvary leaving from the same city gate through which Christ passes in triumph in the *Entry into Jerusalem*. Although the

47

75-77. *Scenes from the Life of Christ: The Entry into Jerusalem; Expulsion of the Moneychangers from the Temple; Judas Receiving Payment for His Betrayal*

scene has certain affinities with some famous fourteenth-century representations of the same subject, like Simone Martini's panel in the Louvre (the similarity is especially close in Christ's backward glance at his mother), the tone is much less emotive.

Some of the most dramatic parts in the *Crucifixion* and the *Lamentation* are played by the small angelic spirits, who appear to have the lower part of their bodies hidden by clouds, a much more effective solution than the one devised for the angelic spirits at

Assisi, whose bodies are merely truncated. These small beings communicate their almost savage desperation through an extraordinary variety of attitudes and facial expressions not given to their human counterparts.

The main figures in the *Lamentation* express their grief with a restraint of gesture reminiscent of the art of antiquity, as can be seen, for instance, in the figure of St. John, bent over with his arms outspread, or the saint on the far right, standing with his arms at his sides and his hands clasped – a gesture which appears in the same scene at Assisi. In this fresco Giotto has abandoned the frenetic movement typical of Byzantine scenes of the Deposition to return to an older, fuller, more solemn expressiveness reminiscent of Greek tragedy. Like an arrow, the rocky ridge in the background descends to indicate the emotional fulcrum of the composition: the juxtaposed heads of Mary and Christ. The figures in this scene have been given a solidity that makes them some of the most impressive in fourteenth-century art.

The dramatic tension of the *Lamentation* is relieved in the more tranquil scene that follows it. In conformity with the Bible, Christ's Resurrection is represented indirectly, through events that bore witness to it – in this case the empty tomb with the two angels and the *Noli me tangere*. The sleeping soldiers gave Giotto the opportunity to do some virtuoso foreshortening, as in the *Resurrection* at Assisi.

The *Ascension* and the *Pentecost* are not among the most famous of the Arena Chapel frescoes, despite their very high quality, and the richness of decoration and color that underlines their spiritual significance. The striking mantle worn by one of the apostles is as magnificent as the gold-trimmed garments of the souls freed from limbo, who ascend into heaven with Christ. It is worth noting that the setting of the

78-81. Scenes from the Life of Christ: The Last Supper; The Washing of Feet; Christ before Caiaphas; The Flagellation

82. Scenes from the Life of Christ: The Kiss of Judas, detail

Pentecost is almost the only one at Padua that directly reflects contemporary Gothic architecture.

The inclusion of the *Seven Virtues* and *Seven Vices* in the chapel decoration was in line with the didactic program of many thirteenth- and fourteenth-century decorative schemes. I have already referred to the novelty of the mock marble dado, a device in keeping with Giotto's conception of architectural illusionism, where these images are inserted as if they were sculptural reliefs. I have also touched upon the prosaic aspect of these works in comparison with the lofty narrative tone of the scenes of the life of

Christ. This prosaic aspect has often been considered a defect, which has in turn led to a certain degree of skepticism over Giotto's authorship. This is probably the result of a commonplace notion that poetry is superior to prose, the tragic to the comic, the sublime to the normal, the solemn to the everyday. Furthermore, there is a mistaken idea that an artist bound to the representation of a set theme is necessarily limited in his freedom of expression, and that his inspiration and the quality of his work are therefore impaired – as if a prescribed theme had prevented Ambrogio Lorenzetti from painting some of the most original frescoes of the whole of the fourteenth century, the *Good and Bad Government* cycle in the Sala della Pace in Siena's Palazzo Pubblico. These works were foreshadowed in the Arena Chapel, in the simulated

*83-85. Scenes from the Life of Christ: The Road to
Calvary; Crucifixion and detail*

bas-relief on the throne of Justice, where the horsemen on the sides and especially the dancers in the middle anticipate features of Lorenzetti's frescoes.

The figures of *Justice* and *Injustice* are larger than those of the other virtues and vices, and occupy a central position on the dado. Both are represented as rulers – Justice wears a royal crown, and Injustice is depicted as a tyrant. Their role as symbols of good and bad government respectively is indicated in the small reliefs on their thrones. Here it is plain that Enrico Scrovegni's political ambitions came into play: the allusion was to the eventuality of his own govern-

ment of the city, a rule that would be based on justice.

The other allegories are perhaps of lesser importance, in spite of the complexity of their symbolism, which is not immediately comprehensible. However, many of these figures have been represented with extraordinary subtlety and delicacy: *Prudence*'s second face, for instance, is represented by the profile of a bearded man at the back of her head.

Each of these figures should be considered first and foremost in its emblematic value, this being the main reason for its inclusion in the decorative scheme, and should always be seen in relation to its opposite. *Prudence*, which also symbolizes the virtue of intelligence, is shown as a mature lady seated at a desk, as if she were a schoolmistress, while her opposite, *Foolishness*, appears as a dimwitted youth dressed as a buffoon. The Herculean *Fortitude* (she

86-89. Scenes from the Life of Christ: Lamentation over the Dead Christ; Noli me tangere; Ascension; Pentecost

90. Scenes from the Life of Christ: Lamentation over the Dead Christ, detail

91-98. *Allegories of the Virtues and the Vices representing: Justice, Injustice, Prudence, Foolishness, Inconstancy, Wrath, Infidelity, Charity*

99. *Last Judgment*

wears a lion skin, the attribute of Hercules) is armed with mace and shield and stands with her feet set firmly on the ground. Her opposite, *Inconstancy*, struggles to maintain her balance as she sits on an unsteady wheel on a sloping floor. *Temperance is* serene and tranquil, while *Wrath* tears the dress from her breast, repeating Caiaphas's gesture of rage before Christ. *Justice* is shown as the personification of prosperity, while the tyrant *Injustice* occupies a crumbling, turreted throne. *Faith*, hieratic in pose, is contrasted with the figure of *Infidelity* (idolatry), who is led on a rope by his female idol, his helmet making him impervious to the word of God from above. The smiling figure of *Charity*, also a symbol of generosity, fecundity and happiness, has her opposite in the grotesque figure of *Envy*. The youthful *Hope* flies upward to receive the crown that awaits her, while *Des-*

peration has hanged herself (note how the pole bends slightly with the weight of her body).

The decorative bands on the walls above contain several scenes from the Old Testament and busts of saints and prophets. The Old Testament scenes are of a very modest standard, and owe their presence in the chapel to the Gothic tradition of representing parallels between the Old and New Testament. Some of the figures of saints and prophets are of very high workmanship and among the most impressive of Giotto's repertoire.

The entrance wall is filled with the imposing *Last Judgment*. This scene is as complex and crowded as the frescoes on the side walls are concentrated and reduced to essentials, and does not give the same impression of order and balance as the others. Indeed, the composition of the various parts of the mystical vision of Judgment Day doubtless presented a serious problem to an artist whose style depended on clarity of both subject and form. The figure of Christ the Judge is enclosed within a mandorla, ringed by angels, which seems to be independent of its surround-

100. Last Judgment, detail showing Enrico Scrovegni presenting the Arena Chapel to the Virgin

ings. It occupies the center of a hollow created by the curve of the ledge supporting the thrones of the twelve apostles (a conception which calls to mind certain late fifteenth- and early sixteenth-century works like Raphael's *Dispute over the Holy Sacrament* in the Stanza della Segnatura in the Vatican). The space is given an impression of even greater depth by the downward slope of the rows of angels above, who look like a heavenly battalion drawn up on parade.

Also noteworthy are the figures of the two angels in the uppermost part of the fresco who roll out the sky as if it were a scroll, revealing the gem-studded walls of the heavenly Jerusalem, as well as the two angels holding the cross below the mandorla and the river of fire that flows from the mandorla down into Hell. The rigid scheme of painting figures on different scales according to their importance does not contribute to a harmonious relationship of parts in a work like this: from the enormous figure of Christ to the Lilliputian figures of the saved and the damned there is a continuous gradation of size which confounds the artist's attempt to instill order into the huge composition.

Yet if we compare this *Last Judgment* with earli-er works like the *Last Judgment* in Sant'Angelo in Formis, the one in Santa Maria Assunta on the island of Torcello or the image in the dome of Florence Baptistery, all of which are divided into a series of independent, horizontal compartments, we can see just how much unity Giotto was able to introduce into this work by eliminating the traditional subdivisions and putting all the groups in the same pictorial space. The fact that the iconographic tradition still exerted a considerable influence is evident in the differentiation of the various groups, but even here Giotto's desire for unity led him to innovate, to make Christ's mandorla a sort of centripetal force toward which the various groups gravitate.

Christ sits within his rainbow-hued mandorla, majestic and commanding, both in pose and scale (though compared to earlier representations he appears human). With his left hand he rejects the damned while, still frowning, he turns his face towards the elect, offering them his right hand. The apostles sit solemnly on their thrones, the richest of which is occupied by Peter. The youthful Virgin, brown-haired and with a gentle face, seems to offer her hand to the first figure in the top row of the elect, probably St. John the Baptist, as if to lead him toward Christ. Unfortunately, this part of the fresco is in very poor condition, and we can barely make out a procession of elders and important personages characterized in the same way as Joachim, the aged Simeon, St. Joseph and the older apostles.

The group of elect immediately below is in a better state of preservation. The figures have not been given haloes, even though they include such important saints as Francis and Dominic and others, like Catherine, who had inspired a vast number of legends. Men and women, laymen and ecclesiastics move in procession towards Christ, accompanied by a row of smiling angels. Their arrangement in parallel lines receding into space gives rise to those curious rows of heads in profile which Giotto relied on to indicate a crowd arranged in orderly fashion in space. The same device was used in the group of kneeling friars in the *Confirmation of the Rule* at Assisi and in the group of apostles in the *Ascension* at Padua.

The damned, who are shown in the lower right hand corner, fall into a Hell dominated by the figure of Satan. This Hell teems with hopeless diminutive figures subjected to a variety of comically indecent humiliations and torments by apish devils. It is a far cry from Dante's tragic vision of Hell and recalls only a few verses of the *Inferno* about the area of Hell known as the Malebolge. Almost all these figures can be attributed to Giotto's assistants, though here, too, the master's guiding hand can be discerned in the rich play of imagination that characterizes the whole and in the execution of certain parts, which suggest his direct intervention. This is true of the wonderfully immediate episode that takes place on the brink of Hell, below the cross, where two devils lead a struggling man back to the damned, dragging him by his clothes, which are pulled over his head to reveal his disproportionate genitals.

Below the cross, on the left, is the dedicatory scene in which Enrico Scrovegni kneels before the Virgin and two saints, offering a model of the Arena Chapel held by an Augustinian friar. The portrait of Scrovegni, who is shown in sharp profile, is a faithful representation of the youthful features of the same man shown in old age on his marble tomb. His clothing and hairstyle reflect the fashions of the day and provide valuable information about contemporary costume. The figure of Scrovegni is on the same scale as the sacred figures he is addressing – evidently it was enough to show him kneeling before these figures to indicate his "inferior" status.

A few decades later Simone Martini was to paint an autonomous portrait at Avignon, although the earliest example of such a picture to have come down to us is the profile of King John the Good of France, now in the Louvre, painted around the middle of the fourteenth century by a French artist. From the fifteenth century onward, this was to become an artistic genre in its own right.

The model of the chapel presented by Scrovegni differs in a few details from the real chapel, a fact which suggests that the *Last Judgment* may have been painted before the exterior of the chapel was completed. This is a strong possibility since the most pictorially advanced parts of the cycle, i.e. those most similar to Giotto's later works, appear on the wall opposite the *Last Judgment,* above and on each side of the chancel arch. The warm, rich colors of the angels surrounding God and the figures of Gabriel and Mary are related to the fresco decorations in the Magdalen Chapel in the Lower Church at Assisi, which are the closest to the Paduan frescoes of all of Giotto's surviving cycles.

The *Crucifix* painted by Giotto for the Arena Chapel (now in the Museo Civico at Padua) also displays a striking similarity to the frescoed *Crucifixion* in the right transept of the Lower Church. But before going on to examine the Lower Church cycle, it is worth lingering for a moment over two works that are closely related in style to the Paduan frescoes, and

which may have been painted a short time before: the *Ognissanti Madonna*, now in the Uffizi, and the *Dormition of the Virgin*, now in the Staatliche Museen of Berlin.

The *Ognissanti Madonna* is the greatest of Giotto's panel paintings. The subject is the same as that of Duccio's *Rucellai Madonna* and Cimabue's *Santa Trinita Madonna*: the enthroned Virgin and Child among saints and angels, facing the observer, and the Child raising his hand in a gesture of benediction. However, much had changed in the few years that separate this work from the others. The sad, remote, inscrutable Virgin of the thirteenth century has been transformed here into a very human woman who gazes serenely outward, her lips parted in a hint of a smile that reveals the white of her teeth. The earthly

101. Crucifix
223x164 cm
Museo Civico, Padua

weight of her body is set off by the delicacy of the Gothic throne, which appears to have undergone the same process of attenuation as the Temple of Minerva in the *Homage of a Simple Man* at Assisi.

In reality what we see here is the juxtaposition of two elements – human figure and architectural object – that are still treated separately, with the same criteria as were used at Assisi.

Compared with similar works by the great painters of the late thirteenth century, this image of the Madonna seems to have been greatly simplified, although by no means impoverished. The cloth of the Virgin's gown and mantle are of the finest quality. The rich coloring of the throne makes it both sumptuous and more convincing than the elaborate structures of thirteenth-century painting. The groups of angels on each side of the throne occupy real space and look like the elegant retainers of a royal court.

The panel of the *Dormition of the Virgin* in Berlin, which was also painted for the church of Ognissanti in Florence, appears to be directly related to the *Ognissanti Madonna*. It has an unusual format and its gabled shape suggests it was meant to be placed above an altarpiece. There are very strong similarities between it and the *Ognissanti Madonna*;

for instance, the angel standing behind the two smaller angels holding candles, on the right, has a profile identical to that of the angel kneeling on the right in the *Ognissanti Madonna*.

The composition is made slightly asymmetrical by the disposition of the group of angels and patriarchs on the right, who form a diagonal rising to a point above Christ's left shoulder. The group on the left forms a similar, lower diagonal which is interrupted by the figure of a young apostle (John?), bending forward and clasping his hands. The simple sarcophagus, ornamented with Cosmatesque decoration, is also asymmetrical, having been set at a slight angle so that both the side and front are visible. The scene represents the moment at which the Virgin's body is lowered into the marble tomb. Angels hold the ends of the shroud, and an apostle is bent over the sarcophagus, supporting the body. In his arms Christ holds an infant in swaddling clothes, a symbol of Mary's soul. As in the Paduan frescoes, the tone is solemn, yet warm and down to earth. Certain parts, such as the angel blowing into the censer and the female figure on the left, who is so covered by her drapery that only a small portion of her profile is visible, anticipate later fourteenth-century painting.

102. Death of the Virgin
75x178 cm
Gemäldegalerie, Berlin

103. Ognissanti Madonna
325x204 cm
Uffizi, Florence

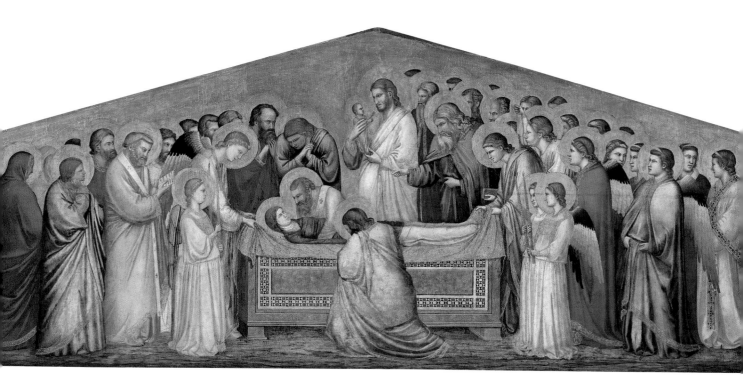

The Lower Church at Assisi

The similarity between the last frescoes to be painted in the Arena Chapel and the frescoes in the chapel of the Magdalen in the Lower Church at Assisi has already been mentioned. The fact that Giotto's assistants were allowed greater freedom in the execution of the Assisi frescoes does not mean that he was not directly involved. There was more wall space at the artists' disposal in the Magdalen Chapel than at Padua, and the two scenes that appear in both places, the *Raising of Lazarus* and *Noli me tangere* are consequently larger and more imposing. The former, in particular, is far more monumental in character than its Paduan counterpart, despite the presence of the same figures in more or less the same attitudes. But because the wall space permitted larger gaps between the figures, Christ's gesture has become more dramatic and the figures of the two Marys more accentuated. If we observe Christ's head we see how much softer and more mel-

low Giotto's painting has grown. The landscape has become gentler, and by comparison the scenery in Padua appears to have much of the harshness of the stony mountains in the *Legend of St. Francis*.

The frescoes on the lower walls of the chapel are enclosed within mock architectural projections supported by lovely twisted columns, and the ones on the upper walls are surrounded by flat decorative borders (as in the Arena Chapel). The chapel houses seven scenes from the life of Mary Magdalene. The narrative starts on the middle row of the left wall, with the *Supper in the House of the Pharisee* (where the saint washes Christ's feet and dries them with her hair), and the *Raising of Lazarus*. It continues on the same level of the right wall, with the *Noli me tangere* (where the

104, 105. Scenes from the Life of the Magdalen: Raising of Lazarus; Noli me tangere

62

resurrected Christ appears to Mary in the guise of a gardener) and the *Miraculous Landing at Marseilles* (Mary Magdalene, Lazarus, Martha and others arrive safely in the French port after having been placed in a rudderless boat by their persecutors). In the lunettes are *Mary Magdalene Speaking to the Angels* (right wall), the *Communion and Ascent into Heaven of Mary Magdalene* (left wall), and *Mary Magdalene and the Hermit Zosimus* (wall above the entrance to the chapel).

Minor frescoes are painted on the soffits of the windows and the two side entrances, while at the sides of the windows, arranged in two rows, are a *Penitent Saint*, *Mary, Sister of Moses* (as we are told by the inscription), *St. Helen*, and a *Martyred Saint*. On the soffit of the entrance are twelve saints, arranged in pairs on three levels: from top left, *Peter and Matthew*, a saint with a cross (Simon of Cyrene?) and one in armor (Longinus?) and two more saints; on the right *Paul and David*, an elderly saint and *Augustine* and another pair of saints. On the lower section of the side walls we see, on the left, *St. Rufinus*, patron of Assisi, with *Bishop Teobaldo Pontano* (who commissioned the chapel and is shown kneeling at the saint's feet) and the *Penitent Magdalen*; on the right, *Mary Magdalene* with *Cardinal Pietro di Barro* and the bust of a saint. On the vault, within four tondi, are set *Christ Giving His Blessing*, *Mary Magdalene*, *Lazarus* and *Martha*.

These frescoes were formerly thought to have been painted after 1314, before it was discovered that Teobaldo Pontano, who commissioned them, did not become bishop of Assisi in that year but in the late thirteenth century. We now know they were executed not long after the Paduan frescoes, probably before 1309 (a recently discovered document mentions that Giotto was in Assisi a short time before that date). The contribution of Giotto's assistants, who were given a free hand here, appears to revert to a pre-Paduan, almost "Master of St. Cecilia" phase of

106, 107. Scenes from the Life of the Magdalen: Mary Magdalene Speaking to the Angels; Mary Magdalene and the Hermit Zosimus

Giotto's development, while the parts where Giotto's own work predominates are characterized by a pictorial and chromatic softness that is much more advanced than at Padua.

The human types found in the Paduan frescoes reappear here, but the colors are warmer and creamier. The dark hair of their Paduan days has turned reddish-blond, and their eyes are often pale. Their features seem more varied and the figures are on a larger scale. The immense rock which dominates the scene of *Mary Magdalene and the Hermit Zosimus* in the lunette above the entrance is as white and soft as a cloud. The bearded profile of the hermit has been rendered with such subtlety that it calls to mind the naturalistic effects that Giottino and Giusto dei Menabuoi were to achieve half a century later.

The angels who bear Mary Magdalene aloft in the scene in the lunette on the right wall have extraordinary faces, with expressions that are much softer than anything seen at Padua. Many of the sacred figures are more imposing and dignified than their Paduan counterparts as well, as is apparent in the splendid group of Christ and Mary in the *Supper in the House of the Pharisee*.

Some of the figures of saints on the soffit, or underside, of the entrance arch are also highly expressive. And in the magnificent dedicatory scene, Mary Magdalene, wearing a pinkish-red dress sumptuously trimmed in gold, takes the hand of Pietro di Barro, who kneels before her. She stands to one side of the large, rectangular fresco, her figure set off by the blue background. The scene is enclosed within a marvelous frame painted to imitate red marble, trimmed in white and ornamented with mock mosaic inlays. At each side is a solid twisted column embellished with a spiraling strip of Cosmati work.

The Magdalen Chapel was the starting point of the work carried out by Giotto and his assistants in the Lower Church, which was to include the right transept and the vault. It has recently been demonstrated that these areas were frescoed before

Pietro Lorenzetti painted the scenes of the Passion in the left transept, executed before 1320. It seems that when the frescoes in the Magdalen Chapel were completed, Giotto and his workshop were asked to redecorate the right transept and vault. This area had been frescoed in the late thirteenth century, as is indicated by Cimabue's large fresco of the *Madonna Enthroned with Angels and St. Francis*, which was spared.

In these frescoes, where Giotto's role was probably that of designer rather than painter, what emerges is the personality of one or two of his assistants – the so-called Relative of Giotto and the Master of the Vaulting Cells – who translated his ideas into their own style. The frescoes include various miracles performed by St. Francis after his death, *St. Francis with a Crowned Skeleton*, a tondo with *Christ Giving His Blessing*, the *Crucifixion* and eight scenes from

the childhood of Christ: the *Visitation*, *Nativity*, *Adoration of the Magi*, *Presentation in the Temple*, *Slaughter of the Innocents*, *Flight into Egypt*, *Christ among the Doctors* and the rare episode of the *Return of the Holy Family to Nazareth*. The rest of the frescoes in the right transept were painted by other artists: Cimabue, the Master of the Chapel of St. Nicholas, Simone Martini and Pietro Lorenzetti.

The frescoes create an impression of splendid chromatic richness. The blues of the backgrounds are the most brilliant in the whole of the fourteenth century. The pinks, whites, yellows and greens are the softest, warmest, densest and brightest in Giotto's palette (it seems as if the walls and the dark tunnel vault of the transept were encrusted with precious stones). Here the artist reveals a capacity for giving concrete form to objects that is reminiscent at times of the extraordinary *trompe-l'œil* effects of the St. Francis cycle. His skilful construction of pictorial space in frescoes such as the *Presentation in the Temple* and *Christ among the Doctors* constitutes perhaps the most advanced use of perspective in the fourteenth century. These frescoes became a model for Umbrian painters of panel pictures, frescoes and miniatures. Proof of their contemporary fame is provided by a few fourteenth-century drawings that have survived, reproducing details from them or whole scenes.

The standard of the frescoes, however, is lower than that of works in which Giotto's participation was more direct. In certain parts we notice a tendency to attenuate the figures, and to refine their features in the Gothic manner. In other parts the wide-eyed figures have the somewhat pathetic look which is first seen in the Lazarus on the vault of the Magdalen Chapel and reappears in the frescoes of the vault.

However, Giotto must have supervised the painting of these frescoes fairly closely as his hand is evident here and there, especially in the sublime *Crucifixion*, which is perhaps the most beautiful, refined, colorful and moving of all his representations of this subject. We have already mentioned the evident similarity of this Christ and the one on the *Crucifix* made for the high altar of the Arena Chapel, a similarity which provides further proof that the Lower Church frescoes were painted not long after those in the Arena Chapel. It has recently been observed that, apart from the figures standing on the right, clearly the work of the Master of the Vaulting Cells, this fresco is entirely by Giotto.

None of his creations is more delicate or more moving than this crucified Christ, whose milky-white body is covered with the marks left his scourging. Only the whites of his lifeless, half-closed eyes are visible. Kneeling at his feet, on the right, are three Franciscans whose features are so lifelike that they could almost have been painted by Masaccio. They are portraits even more intense and individualized than that of Enrico Scrovegni at Padua. The three solemn mourners standing on the left, St. John and the two Marys, reveal their grief through beautifully modulated gestures and an expressiveness that ranges from the

112, 113. Scenes from the Life of Christ: Crucifixion and detail

114. Vault with the Franciscan Allegories

quiet weeping of St. John to the scream of the beautiful, ardent Mary and Mary Magdalene's grimace of pain. The small angelic spirits are borne by cloudlets that seem to have suddenly materialized on the blue background. Their profound expressiveness has been united with a solidity of form and an articulation of features that is rendered with great freedom yet admirable control.

When the right transept was finished, Giotto's team of painters went on to fresco the vault above the high altar. In the most striking of these frescoes, *St. Francis in Glory*, gold leaf has been used lavishly in the embroidery on the saint's clothing and in the background. Though common in panel paintings, the use of gold in a fresco was unusual, considering the cost of the material and the scale of the undertaking. The fact that the fresco decorations in the Lower Church reach the height of their magnificence in the

vault bears witness to the prevailing tendency of the Franciscan movement at the time: a rejection of the basic tenet of poverty preached by the order's founder. The emergence of this trend, particularly from the time of the generalship of Giovanni da Murro, is reflected in the increasing splendor of the fresco decorations of the basilica of San Francesco, which is evident if we compare the Upper and Lower Church.

The vault contains four complicated Franciscan allegories: *St. Francis in Glory*, the *Allegory of Obedience*, the *Allegory of Chastity* and the *Allegory of Poverty*. Filled with smiling, joyful figures, they are painted in the same style as the scenes from Christ's childhood in the right transept. The hand of the assistant traditionally known as the Master of the Vaulting Cells, whose style is characterized by the astonished expressions of his figures, predominates in these frescoes.

The Peruzzi Chapel

It is difficult to say what degree of affinity there is between the new style of Giotto's workshop and the decoration of the Peruzzi Chapel in Santa Croce, which was probably carried out not long after the works described above. There is reason to believe that the *Kress Collection Polyptych* (Raleigh, North Carolina), which includes *Christ Giving His Blessing*, the *Virgin*, *St. Francis*, and the two *St. Johns*, to whom the chapel was dedicated, is the lost altarpiece of the Peruzzi Chapel. Whether this is true or not, it must be admitted that the figure of Christ has close links with the *Christ Giving His Blessing* in the tondo above one of the entrances to the right transept of the Lower Church. However, the quality of this "slavishly Giottesque" polyptych,

as it has been described, leaves one reluctant to accept that Giotto was directly involved in its execution.

Unfortunately the Peruzzi cycle was extensively repainted, and what remains of the original frescoes, revealed during a recent restoration, is in a poor state of preservation. There is still much controversy over the dating of this chapel and that of the Bardi family adjoining it, but the author favors a date of between 1310 and 1316.

The cycle consists of scenes from the lives of St. John the Baptist (left wall) and St. John the Evangelist (right wall): the *Annunciation to Zacharias*, the *Birth and Naming of the Baptist*, the *Feast of Herod* (including the episode of Salome giving John the Baptist's head to her mother), *St. John on Patmos*, the *Raising of Drusiana* and the *Ascension of the Evangelist*. The small heads framed by hexagons are the most interesting of the minor paintings. They are so lifelike and individualized that they are thought to be portraits of members of the Peruzzi family.

The frescoes were planned on an exceptionally large scale. In this respect the cycle would appear to be a continuation of experiments begun in the chapel of the Magdalen (the Evangelist in the *Raising of Drusiana* is strongly reminiscent of Christ in the *Resurrection of Lazarus* at Assisi). The large areas of wall in the Peruzzi Chapel permitted a far greater pictorial complexity than did those of the Arena Chapel, and consequently the majestic figures that populate the frescoes and the architectural structures in which they move so convincingly are grander than anything at Assisi. As the chapel is very high, fairly long and narrow, Giotto employed

an oblique rather than frontal point of view, imagining the observer would be standing at the chapel entrance. Consequently, the buildings are set at an angle, so that the side nearest the entrance is visible.

The relationship of figure and architecture has become much more harmonious than at Padua, and each architectural structure has more than enough room for the figures it contains. In the *Raising of Drusiana*, the architectural backdrop formed by the walls of an Eastern city is perfectly coherent (no longer the series of separate boxes seen in the Assisi frescoes), and is on approximately the same scale as the figures. The orderly, well-constructed space evident in the *Feast of Herod* and the *Ascension of St. John the Evangelist* was to be adopted by Maso di Banco, one of Giotto's greatest followers, whose work can be seen in the Bardi di Vernio Chapel in Santa Croce.

However, our judgment of the Peruzzi Chapel frescoes has to remain suspended. It is difficult to envisage their original splendor, and to gauge how much they reflected Giotto's new style. We can only admire the single well-preserved fragment in the chapel, the

hand of St. John the Evangelist in the scene where he resuscitates Drusiana. It is a work of such strength that we are reminded of Masaccio, and regret deeply the almost total loss of these frescoes.

According to Ghiberti, Giotto decorated four chapels in Santa Croce and painted altarpieces for each chapel. A group of paintings probably executed between the decoration of the Peruzzi and Bardi Chapels may have constituted one of these altarpieces. It consists of seven square panels (average size 45 x 44 cm) representing the *Adoration of the Magi* (Metropolitan Museum, New York), the *Presentation in the Temple* (Gardner Museum, Boston), the *Last Supper* and the *Crucifixion* (both in the Alte Pinakothek, Munich), the *Entombment* (Berenson Collection, Settignano), the *Descent into Limbo* (Munich), and the *Pentecost* (National Gallery, London). The presence of St. Francis in the group of figures kneeling at the foot of the cross in the *Crucifixion*, which must have been the central panel, suggests that the work was done for a Franciscan church or chapel.

Although the poor state of preservation of the

71

119. Deposition
44.5x43 cm
Berenson Collection,
Settignano (Florence)

120. Last Supper
42.5x43.2 cm
Alte Pinakothek, Munich

121. Pentecost
45x44 cm
National Gallery, London

panels makes their assessment somewhat difficult, Giotto's participation in their execution cannot be doubted. His hand is especially evident in the *Last Supper*, which bears a direct relation, even in the faces of the apostles, to the same scene in the Arena Chapel, while the gallery running along the wall echoes the idea used in the *Marriage at Cana*. The construction of the work is so carefully studied that one suspects that the small hole visible in the center of the panel was made by a nail placed there to secure a string used to draw the perspective lines, a practice that was to become common among the fresco painters of the fifteenth century.

The *Christ Crucified* in the central panel appears to be closely related to the large painted *Crucifix* in San Felice, Florence, a work whose high quality is more apparent now that restoration has freed the surface of its thick layer of dirt. The early date of the San Felice work is revealed not only by its simple rectilinear shape, but also by the weight of Christ's body, which recalls the early *Crucifix* in Santa Maria Novella.

The poorly-preserved *Crucifix* in the Louvre and the one in the church of Ognissanti in Florence must have been painted much later. The elegance and pathos of the latter reveal its affinities with the frescoes in the right transept and on the ceiling of the Lower Church at Assisi.

The most important of Giotto's later panel paintings is the *Stefaneschi Altarpiece*, executed for the high altar of St. Peter's in Rome and mentioned as a work of his in the obituary of Cardinal Jacopo Stefaneschi, who commissioned the work. It is a double-sided triptych and has been preserved almost in its entirety (only two of the three panels of the back predella are missing). It is in the Pinacoteca Vaticana and was recently cleaned.

The scenes on the altarpiece are dominated by the solemn, sacramental tone of the central panel on each side: a tone which, precisely because it is unusual in Giotto's work, demonstrates his ability to adapt his art to the requirements of each new commission. On the front of the central panel Christ sits on his throne, raising his right hand in a gesture of benediction and holding the Book of Revelations in his left. As in thirteenth-century paintings of the *Maestà*, the throne is surrounded by a group of angels, but here their slightly circular disposition has been subtly adapted. Cardinal Stefaneschi is shown kneeling in the foreground. The crucifixion of St. Peter is depicted on the left panel and the beheading of St. Paul on the right. The predella shows the enthroned Madonna, flanked by two angels and the twelve apostles, standing. The predella figures have a detached, arcane air, one that calls to mind the rows of saints in Byzantine mosaics.

The central panel on the back of the altarpiece shows St. Peter enthroned in the same pose as Christ (he is in fact the Vicar of Christ), flanked by two angels and Sts. George and Sylvester. The figures kneeling in the foreground are Celestine V, canonized in 1313, and Cardinal Stefaneschi, who is offering a model of the altarpiece. Attention has often been drawn to the singularity of this last detail, which has been conceived with such naturalistic acumen that it calls to mind Flemish painting. On each of the side panels are the solemn figures of two standing apostles.

As a whole, the *Stefaneschi Altarpiece* is of high standard, and certain parts are remarkable in both conception and execution. This is true, for instance, of the episode of the beheading of St. Paul on the far left of the scene, where the very tall Plautilla, standing on a rock, stretches out her hands to receive the cloth – dropped by the saint when he was taken up to Heaven by the angels – as it floats earthward. The perfect harmony of space and volume (especially in the scene of St. Peter enthroned and the predella scene of the Madonna), the richness of color, the subtle Gothic refinement of some of the figures and the enchanting, enigmatic expressions of others closely link this complex work to the frescoes in the Lower Church. We also notice here that the draped female figure shown in profile on the left of the decapitation scene has been represented in the same attitude as Mary standing behind St. John in the *Crucifixion* at Assisi.

*122. Crucifix
343x432 cm
San Felice
in Piazza,
Florence*

123, 124.
Front and
back of the
Stefaneschi
Altarpiece
Pinacoteca
Vaticana

The Bardi Chapel

There are two fine if badly-preserved panel paintings of the *Crucifixion* which appear to have a close affinity with the *Stefaneschi Altarpiece* in their delicate proportions, rich colors and pathos. One is a gabled panel in the Staatliche Museen of Berlin, the other a rectangular panel in the Musées Municipaux of Strasbourg. The latter forms a diptych with the Wildenstein *Madonna Enthroned with Saints and Virtues*, a work which can be attributed with some certainty to the Master of the Vaulting Cells. The novelty of these Crucifixions consists in the treatment of the crowd at the foot of the cross: one gets the impression that the picture frame has abruptly cut off a small portion of an immense crowd. A subtle innovation in the Strasbourg panel is the reduction in scale of the horsemen, who thus appear to be on a different plane and at a greater distance from the figures in the foreground. The broad sweep of St. John's mantle as he raises his hands to his face has so pure a rhythm that it calls to mind Greek stelae. In both paintings Christ's body has become elongated. This Christ is far removed from the realism of the one in the Santa Maria Novella *Crucifix*.

This new Gothic tendency characterizes much of Giotto's late work, which is best represented by the frescoes in the Bardi Chapel of Santa Croce. By then the great Sienese painter Simone Martini had developed a refined and sophisticated version of Giotto's art, one deeply influenced by the French Gothic style. He was fast becoming Giotto's most serious Italian rival (he, too, was receiving many commissions from abroad), and Giotto's response to Martini's success

125.
St. Stephen
84x54 cm
Museo Horne,
Florence

126.
Crucifixion
39x26 cm
Musées
Municipaux,
Strasbourg

was to modify his own painting, making it more refined and ornate.

The partially reconstructed polyptych consisting of the *Madonna and Child* (National Gallery, Washington), *St. Stephen* (Museo Horne, Florence) and *Sts. John the Evangelist and Lawrence* (Musée Jacquemart-André, Châalis) is so close stylistically to the Bardi Chapel frescoes that some of the faces seem to be almost interchangeable. Although they have the solemn bearing found in all of Giotto's large-scale paintings, the figures in these panels are distinguished by their aura of luxury and wealth. The *Madonna*, who has the long narrow eyes of her counterpart on a French ivory, seems to have arrayed herself magnificently in a mantle whose folds anticipate the impression of warm, velvety luxury created by certain of Gentile da Fabriano's paintings. St. Stephen is dressed in a sumptuously ornate dalmatic and carries a richly bound book. Even though the tone is not as exquisitely worldly and courtly as that of a Simone Martini painting, one feels that Giotto intended these panels to challenge his young Sienese rival.

The Bardi Chapel frescoes did not provide the opportunity for such richness, given the rule of poverty imposed by St. Francis. However, the elongated figures, delicate colors and pictorial softness are in keeping with the tendency described above. The characters in the scenes from the life of St. Francis, again shown in contemporary dress given their close proximity in time, have been given a more earthy, realistic appearance than those in the Peruzzi Chapel. The St. Francis cycle at Assisi still served as the model for the scenes from his life, though the limited space in the chapel made it necessary to restrict the number of episodes represented.

The *Renunciation of Worldly Goods* appears in the lunette of the left wall and the *Confirmation of the Rule* in the lunette on the opposite wall. *St. Francis before the Sultan* and the *Apparition at Arles* are set immediately below them. At the bottom of the left wall we see the *Death and Ascension of St. Francis*, while the *Vision of the Ascension of St. Francis* is on the opposite wall. *St. Francis Receiving the Stigmata* is painted on the outer wall above the entrance arch. Only three of the original four Franciscan saints represented next to the window have survived: *Louis of Toulouse*, *Clare* and the badly damaged *Elizabeth of Hungary*. The painted tondi on the vault enclose poorly preserved allegorical figures: *Chastity*, *Poverty* and *Obedience*; the fourth tondo has not survived.

The Bardi Chapel was completely whitewashed in the eighteenth century, as was the Peruzzi Chapel, and tombs were built against its walls, destroying parts of the frescoes. The frescoes were uncovered in 1852, the missing parts filled in and the whole surface repainted. When the repainting was removed by the Florentine

127. *View of the Bardi Chapel Santa Croce, Florence*

128. *Scenes from the Life of St. Francis: The Appearance to Brother Agostino and the Bishop of Assisi, detail Santa Croce, Florence*

Fine Arts Service in 1958-59, the original frescoes reemerged in fair condition, save for the unsightly gaps.

We know from both contemporary sources and thirteenth-century paintings that St. Francis was bearded, yet he appears without one in the Bardi Chapel frescoes. This iconographical irregularity is doubtless linked to the revisionist current in the Franciscan movement, represented by the Conventuals, and to subsequent attempts to modify the image of the most popular saint in Christendom, a change that

129-131. Scenes from the Life of St. Francis:
The Renunciation of Worldly Goods; The Ordeal by Fire
before the Sultan; The Funeral of St. Francis
Santa Croce, Florence

involved not only denying his traditional association with poverty but also his physical appearance. At a time when beards were regarded with distaste by members of polite society, a subtle intention lay hidden in the omission of St. Francis' beard, an iconographical deviation that originated in the papacy toward the end of the thirteenth century.

The Bardi Chapel frescoes condense the saint's life into a series of representative events: his renunciation of worldly goods, papal recognition of the Franciscan Order, his vocation as missionary to the East (at the time of the Crusades), a miracle performed during his lifetime, the appearance of the stigmata and two miracles performed after his death. The plan differed from that of the Peruzzi frescoes in that the

observer was envisaged as standing approximately in the center of the chapel, facing either of the side walls. The arrangement of the scenes on different levels was taken into account and the buildings in the uppermost scenes accordingly foreshortened. This is evident in the splendid construction in the background of the *Renunciation of Worldly Goods*, which was to provide a rich source for Giotto's faithful follower, Taddeo Gaddi, whose studies of oblique buildings were to culminate in the magnificent structure in the *Presentation in the Temple* in the Baroncelli Chapel of the same church. Just as the Peruzzi frescoes were important to the formation of Maso di Banco, the ones in the Bardi Chapel greatly influenced the development of Gaddi, who drew inspiration from them for a series of scenes from the life of St. Francis he painted on the panel of a cabinet door in the sacristy of Santa Croce (now in the Galleria dell'Accademia, Florence). He was also to remain faithful – to the very end of his long career – to the robust but long-limbed figures of the Bardi Chapel frescoes. The *Confirmation of the Rule* was the direct source of Giovanni da Milano's *Expulsion of Joachim from the Temple*, a solemn symmetrical construction of buildings and figures painted in the Rinuccini Chapel of Santa Croce around 1365.

The St. Francis cycle in the Bardi Chapel lacks the liveliness of its Assisi counterpart, and gives the impression of being separated from us in time by a curtain of sanctity. Yet certain features, like the angry father in the *Renunciation of Worldly Goods* and the figure of St. Anthony in the *Apparition at Arles*, were clearly inspired by the Assisi cycle. The scenes here are much more unified and symmetrical, the paint is full and velvety, the colors light and delicate. Clarity and order are still the fundamental principles. Notice the careful arrangement of the friars behind St. Francis in the *Confirmation of the Rule* and the balanced composition of the *Apparition at Arles*, which is prevented from being monotonous by devices such as the row of heads placed behind the low dividing wall to suggest greater depth, the inclusion of the marvelous figure of the young friar absorbed in thought and the gradual darkening of the shadow cast by the roof on the white wall, which produces an effect so subtle that it anticipates Fra Angelico's fresco of the *Annunciation*, painted over a century later, in one of the cells of San Marco.

We cannot help but admire the balance maintained between the studied precision of the composition and the eloquent expression of grief in the *Death and Ascension of St. Francis*, where a small group of friars is gathered round the pale figure of the dead saint, expressing their profound sorrow with great dignity. A comparison of this scene with the Paduan *Lamentation* clarifies the distinction that Giotto intended to maintain – to speak in Dantesque terms – between the "tragic" level of the life of Christ as told in the Bible and the "comic" level of the legend of an almost contemporary saint.

The presence of Louis of Toulouse among the saints represented at the sides of the window provides one indication of the date of the Bardi frescoes, as they cannot have been painted before 1317, the year he was canonized. The stylistic similarity of these frescoes to Giotto's last works, and even to the frescoes in the Bargello Chapel in Florence, which were completed by his workshop a few months after his death, place them at a late stage of the artist's career.

In the last years of his life Giotto's energies were divided between his role as master builder of Florence Cathedral (this was when he began work on the Campanile, known as "Giotto's Tower") and prestigious commissions throughout Italy (between 1329 and 1333 he was working in Naples for Robert of Anjou;

in about 1335, according to Villani, he was in Milan, working for Azzone Visconti). But he still found time to oversee the activity of his efficient workshop, which was producing ambitious, richly colored works such as the *Bologna Polyptych* (executed for the church of Santa Maria degli Angeli and now in the Pinacoteca) and the altarpiece in the Baroncelli Chapel of Santa Croce, both of which bear his signature.

Flanked by four stern saints, the Madonna of the *Bologna Polyptych* sits on a throne that is the most Gothic of all the thrones painted by Giotto. She has the demeanor of an elegant, almost worldly lady. The lovely decorations and the brilliant, shimmering colors contribute to the richness of this work. The resplendent *Coronation of the Virgin* in the Baroncelli Chapel, which cannot have been decorated before the end of the 1320s, is undoubtedly one of Giotto's last great conceptions. The neat, colorful rows of beatific souls on the side panels suggest that Paradise is a place of perfect order – and perspective! One feels that the side panels could continue into infinity, making it a boundless Paradise. In contrast, the central panel with the elegant figures of Christ and the Virgin has something of the refined worldliness of a court ceremony.

Giotto's influence on the frescoes in the Bargello Chapel is most evident in the scene of the *Last Judgment* on the back wall (although badly deteriorated, we can still make out a few beautifully painted heads of the blessed). He died in early 1337, before the frescoes had been completed. He had followed a path which led from the revolutionary vitality of the frescoes in the Upper Church at Assisi, through the more serene classical narrative of the Arena Chapel frescoes, to the warm chromatic frescoes of his second sojourn at Assisi, the starting point for his last, refined Gothic period.

In his lifetime Giotto had raised painting to a prestigious level among the arts, to such an extent that it now influenced sculpture rather than the other way round, as is demonstrated by the work of the great Andrea Pisano. Italian painting can be said to have changed more radically with the appearance of Giotto than ever before. The impulse that Giotto gave to the arts was so great that it shaped the destiny of European painting. By the middle of the fourteenth century the rest of Europe had already become aware of Giotto's innovations, which accorded with the growing secular tendency in European society. His rediscovery of the third dimension, of real and measurable space, of the natural appearance of surfaces, of the individualizing aspects of reality, all this became the heritage of European art, which turned to the figurative world of Italy with ever growing curiosity. And there can be no doubt that the great reform carried out by Jan van Eyck in the Flemish painting of the fifteenth century had its deepest roots in Giotto's revolution.

132. *Bologna Polyptych*
91x340 cm
Pinacoteca Nazionale, Bologna

133. *Baroncelli Altarpiece*
185x323 cm
Santa Croce, Florence